Remembering the DERBY

1948 Triple Crown champion Citation, with Eddie Arcaro up.
(Courtesy Keeneland-Cook)

Remembering the DERBY

Jim Bolus

PELICAN PUBLISHING COMPANY
Gretna 1994

Library of Congress Cataloging-in-Publication Data

Bolus, Jim.
    Remembering the Derby / Jim Bolus.
        p.   cm.
    ISBN 1–56554–040–9
    1. Kentucky Derby, Louisville, Ky.—Anecdotes.
I. Title.
    SF357.K4B635 1994
    798.4'009769'44—dc20   93–34923
                                                                      CIP

Manufactured in the United States of America
Published by Pelican Publishing Company
1101 Monroe Street, Gretna, Louisiana 70053

To Suzanne,
my best friend

Contents

Acknowledgments

Just as I did with *Kentucky Derby Stories*, I first wish to acknowledge my indebtedness to Judy Bortner, director of retail operations for the Kentucky Derby Museum. Without her suggesting my name to Pelican Publishing Company, neither *Kentucky Derby Stories* nor *Remembering the Derby* would ever have gotten off and running.

Special thanks also goes to head librarian Doris Waren and associate librarian Cathy Schenck at the Keeneland Library. They have always been my right hand in researching horse racing.

I also thank the entire staffs at Churchill Downs and the Kentucky Derby Museum. Thanks, too, to the Kentucky Racing Commission, the University Archives and Records Center at the University of Louisville, the Louisville Free Public Library, the Kentucky Thoroughbred Owners and Breeders, *The Blood-Horse*, the New York Racing Association press office, The Jockey Club, and the Douglas (Wyoming) Area Chamber of Commerce.

Books that have served as research sources include *Run for the Roses*, *The Kentucky Derby Diamond Jubilee*, *Shoemaker*, *Down the Stretch*, *The Great Ones*, *Miss Elizabeth Arden*, *The Most Glorious Crown*, various issues of *The American Racing Manual*, and *Training for Fun, and Profit—Maybe!*

Many publications have been used through the years in researching the chapters that appear in this book, including *The Courier-Journal*, *The Blood-Horse* magazine, *Lexington Herald-Leader*, *The New York Times*, the *San Francisco*

9

Examiner, Thoroughbred Times, Keeneland magazine, *Daily Racing Form, The Saturday Evening Post, The Florida Horse, Business First, Daily Herald, Kansas City Star, Los Angeles Times, Racing Post, Louisville Daily Sports News,* New Orleans *Times-Picayune, 1987 Kentucky Derby Souvenir Magazine, 1988 Kentucky Derby Souvenir Magazine, Turf and Sport Digest, The Thoroughbred of California, Life* magazine, and *Sports Illustrated,* as well as such now-defunct publications as the *Kentucky Irish American, The Thoroughbred Record* (formerly the *Kentucky Live Stock Record* and later the *Live Stock Record), Thoroughbred Racing Action, New York World, The Louisville Times, Kentucky Inter-Track News, The Louisville Commercial, Spirit of the Times,* and the *Goodwin's, Krik's,* and *Watson's* racing guides.

For photographs, I wish to thank Churchill Downs Incorporated/Kinetic Corporation, Amy Petit at the Keeneland Association, Andy Belfiore at the New York Racing Association, Santa Anita Park, Rick Buckley, Dan Farley, Russ Harris, the Thoroughbred Racing Associations, Stidham & Associates, and my favorite photographer—longtime friend Dick Martin.

Hundreds of people have assisted me and been patient with me over the years, and there isn't enough space to list them all. I would be remiss in not mentioning Tom Meeker, Bernie Hettel, Jerry Botts, Dave Hooper, Keene Daingerfield, Joe Hirsch, Nick Clarke, Pat Eddery, Logan Bailey, Jack Price, Charles Taylor, Bernard McCormack, Joe Hickey, Ric Waldman, Mrs. Fred Hooper, Pat Basile, Steve DiMauro, Dr. Gary Lavin, Dr. Dave Richardson, W. C. ("Woody") Stephens, Barney Bright, Preston Madden, Gordon Turner, Ron McAnally, George Koper, Joe Burnham, Tony Rau, Frank Tours, Eddie Arcaro, Margaret Glass, Jean Cruguet, Harvey Vanier, Cap Hershey, Don DeWitt, Dan Farley, Cliff Guilliams, Russ Harris, Earl Ruby, Christopher Poole, George Ennor, J. Simpson Dean,

Peggy Lacy Moore, Ina Duncan, Sal Tufano, and his son, Sal.

And, finally, I need to give special thanks to Suzanne, my best friend, my adviser, my typist, my proofreader . . . and my wife of twenty-nine years.

Introduction

In trying to put together another book on the favorite Kentucky Derby stories that I have written over the years, I naturally resurrected (and added to) a piece that I had done on Mike Barry, the wittiest newspaperman I've ever known. Barry loved the Derby, and some of his best writing came at Derby time when he would take great joy in commenting on the starters before or after the race. In 1974, his "alibi" for Consigliori was priceless. And in 1981, his comment on Partez was a gem. (I won't tell you what he said here; you'll have to turn to "The Best of Mike Barry on the Derby.")

I've devoted chapters to Keene Daingerfield, the most respected racing official I've ever met; and Joe Hirsch, the most respected racing writer in the history of the business. Joe is the person directly responsible for my interest in Derby history, and I have always been indebted to him for what he's done for me. If not for Joe and his support, I doubt that I would ever have written a book on the Derby. Now I have written four, including one with him, and it is truly my privilege to call him a friend.

I've also written a chapter on W. C. ("Woody") Stephens, one of the most knowledgeable trainers in the history of the game. Stephens won the 100th running of the Kentucky Derby with Cannonade in 1974, and then ten years later he saddled another Derby winner in Swale. A chapter doesn't begin to tell the story about Stephens' many accomplishments. A book already has been written about him,

Jack Price with Carry Back in 1969. (Photo by Jim Bolus)

but what Hollywood needs to do someday is make a movie on the life of this great horseman.

One chapter deals with Silky Sullivan, the twelfth-place finisher in the 1958 Derby. Never has one horse done so little in the Derby to warrant so much coverage. Silky Sullivan beat just two horses, one of whom was eased. Even so, that Derby will always be known as "Silky's Derby."

Chapters are also devoted to such personalities as Fred Hooper, Elizabeth Arden Graham, and Ed Corrigan.

I've also written a chapter on Sir Barton. In 1976, I visited Sir Barton's grave in Douglas, Wyoming. Sir Barton faded away from the spotlight and he wound up his days in Wyoming, where he is buried; but in 1919, he was a famous horse, winning the three races that later became known as the Triple Crown.

There's a chapter called "Diary of a Derby Winner," which covers Affirmed's road to success in 1978. The 1978 Derby was one of the most memorable I've ever covered.

This book contains other chapters, and I hope you enjoy them.

As I have previously written, nobody has ever succeeded in putting into words what the Derby is all about, and this book doesn't pretend to tell the story of the race from beginning to end. As was the case with *Kentucky Derby Stories*, this book is just a collection of my favorite stories about my favorite sporting event—the Kentucky Derby.

I have always thoroughly enjoyed researching and studying this grand old race. I hope you agree with me that it's a fascinating subject . . . the Kentucky Derby.

Remembering
the DERBY

Mike Barry had the following tip for those attending the races: "*Never bet on a horse that can't pass the 1–4–1 Test—one head, four legs, one tail.*" *He maintained that his bad handicapping was so* "*renowned*" *that* "*when I went into the service in 1940, they only asked me to do one thing for my country: Pick Japan.*" (Photo by Bill Straus, courtesy Keeneland Association)

1

The Best of Mike Barry on the Derby

WHEN MIKE BARRY WAS TWELVE YEARS OLD, he saw his first Kentucky Derby. That would be 1922, back when knicker-bockers were in style, the kind of knee pants that Barry wore on the day he went to Churchill Downs to watch the forty-eighth Derby.

Years later, Barry would delight in telling the story about how he—as a "smart-aleck kid" watching the race from the infield—declared before the field had gone a quarter of a mile that the favored Morvich would never last on the front end. Morvich, of course, did last the Derby distance, and Barry liked to poke fun at himself for being so wrong at his first Derby.

Barry saw sixty-six runnings of this world-famous race, many of them from the press box as first a writer for the *Kentucky Irish American*, then *The Louisville Times* and, later in retirement, as secretary-treasurer of the National Turf Writers Association. He died on January 10, 1992, at the age of eighty-two, leaving a legacy of great Derby writing.

A witty writer who rarely lacked for an opinion, Barry knew the Derby the way few journalists have ever known it. Let's go back through the years and reread Barry at his best.

1948—This was the year of a Triple Crown winner, Ci-tation, who ran with Coaltown in the Derby in a heavily favored Calumet Farm entry.

"Yeah, a pushover Derby," Barry wrote in *Kentucky Irish American.* "All a guy has to do is pick against Citation—or against Coaltown. As a young 3-year-old, Citation beat the best older horses, the acid test of true class. In his first stakes race, Coaltown beat a fine field of older sprinters. Then, with only three six-furlong races under his belt, his first effort over a route broke a track record. How good IS this horse?

"The safe pick is to take Citation, the known quantity. Win or lose, you'll know you picked a fine horse.

"I can't play it safe. I honestly believe Coaltown is going to win the Derby, and that's the way I've got to go."

After Citation won the Derby, Barry wrote: "Good old Count Fleet! If it hadn't been for this long-shot [2.80] winner I stabbed in 1943, my Derby record would now be 15 losers in 15 years. As it is, I've only had 14 out of 15.

"You've got to admit I'm getting better, too. Last year my Phalanx missed only by a head, and last Saturday Coaltown was nosed out by a mere 3½ lengths. Some people are saying the result would have been different if Jockey Pierson had urged Coaltown a little more vigorously. I must agree with these people. Had Pierson really booted the colt, I don't think Citation would have beaten him by more than 3¼ lengths.

"Citation—well, he's everything they say, and more."

Indeed, Barry would later call Citation the best horse he ever saw.

1953—"I don't think Native Dancer is going to be beaten fair and square, and I don't want to see him lose through bad racing luck," Barry wrote. "I think Native Dancer will win, and win easily."

Native Dancer lost by a head to Dark Star, a defeat that would prove to be the only blemish in his twenty-two career starts. Native Dancer was bumped on the clubhouse turn, and the *Daily Racing Form* chart caller went so far as to say that he was "probably best."

Barry had an opinion on the race himself, saying: "I thought Native Dancer was the best, but not much the best. Even with the clearest of sailing, he wouldn't have beaten Dark Star by much more than the winner beat him. The interference Native Dancer suffered at the clubhouse turn has been greatly exaggerated—I've seen many horses recover from much worse and go on to win."

1956—"Besomer is a son of Double Jay, who finished 12th in 1947. He may do better, say 11th.

"No Regrets beat two horses in the Trial. I wouldn't be surprised if he beat three in the Derby."

"Jean Baptiste came a long way to take a beating."

"Black Emperor will abdicate after a mile."

Barry's Derby forecast: Needles, Count Chic, High King, Terrang, Countermand. Of Needles, Barry wrote: "He's the only horse in the race who's looked like a Derby horse all the way."

Tips from others in the family: "My brother Joe predicts Count Chic, Fabius, Needles," Barry wrote. "My wife's going to bet on Countermand. With, I hope, her money."

Following Needles' triumph, Barry wrote: "I had my first Derby winner in thirteen years, and it was a wonderful, wonderful feeling."

1958—". . . here's my guess: Tim Tam, Jewel's Reward, Silky Sullivan, Jet's Alibi."

Barry was right about this Derby, which was won by Tim Tam. But he was wrong about controversial jockey Bill Hartack, and he admitted so the week after the Derby.

"It's a pleasure to stand corrected," Barry wrote. "According to the veteran C-J turf writer Bill Surface, who's been around at least two years, Willie Hartack isn't the ill-mannered, obnoxious punk I've thought.

"He's a fine, upstanding, clean-living, unafraid American boy, always ready with a polite answer to a polite question.

"Sweet William merely objects to 'stupid questions from phonies.'

"It's just unfortunate that Sweet William has to encounter so many phonies among the members of the working press, all of whom seem to be burdened with stupid questions.

"Perhaps we can all learn from Surface. In the future we should approach Sweet William in the proper bent posture, all puckered up, and who knows? He might even give us that boyish smile as he spits in our eye."

1959—Not only did Barry pick Derby winner Tomy Lee, but he even correctly told the reader how the race would be won. "Shoemaker to rate him on or near the pace, then keep him going through that long stretch," he wrote.

Shoemaker did just that, keeping Tomy Lee going with a brilliant ride to edge Sword Dancer by a nose.

Barry also was right about Troilus, picking him to finish last. "Didn't like him when he was winning," Barry wrote. "All I feel for him now is pity. In his present condition, [he] has no business in this race."

And, of Die Hard, he wrote: "This is what you've got to be to stay with this one. Has everything except speed and stamina."

The next week in the *Kentucky Irish American*, under the heading of "The Customers Always Write," Barry wrote:

"It's a good thing some of my friends were nice enough to write, even if what they wrote wasn't particularly nice. I'm stymied myself. Writing long alibis after my horses lose is easy—I've had years of experience—but commenting on winners is something strange.

"Besides, I'm still in shock. Therefore let's let the clients take over."

From Clara Allen: "Now you really are on my list. It's true I seldom know which horse to bet on, but I always before have known which one NOT to bet on. You let me down—and in the Derby race at that."

To which Barry replied: "Think of it this way, Clara. I did you a favor. One more successful year of betting against my selection would have put you in a higher bracket."

From Joe Dumesnil, Jr.: "May I extend my congratulations for not only picking Tomy Lee but also describing Shoemaker's ride in advance."

Barry's reply: "Thanks, but I can't help thinking you must be new around here. I should also point out that my descriptions of rides after the numbers go up are much more colorful."

1960—Barry's pre-Derby comments included these words of encouragement for those wishing to wager on:

Lurullah—"A well-bred bum."

Spring Broker—"Won his last start at Sportsman's Park. Should never have left."

Barry's prediction, in order of finish: Bally Ache, Venetian Way, Tompion, Victoria Park, Tony Graff, Cuvier Relic, Divine Comedy, Spring Broker, Bourbon Prince, Lurullah, Yomolka, Fighting Hodge, and Henrijan.

He had the two finishers on the front end reversed—Venetian Way won and Bally Ache ran second—but he was right on the back end. "I have finally discovered the best system for picking the Derby," Barry wrote. "Just start with the last horse and work up. In 1959 I gave you Troilus to finish 17th and last, which he did, and this year I correctly predicted that Henrijan would trail the first dozen."

Another post-Derby observation from Barry:

"A favorite adjective applied to Churchill Downs—both *Sports Illustrated* and Red Smith used it last week—is ramshackle.

"Webster says ramshackle means 'tumbling down, shaky, in need of repair.'

"I suggest that Churchill Downs is none of these.

"I suggest they all get a new word."

1961—Barry picked Flutterby to win the Derby, with Crozier second and Carry Back third. Carry Back, trailing by more than thirteen lengths with a quarter of a mile to go, triumphed by three-quarters of a length over Crozier. Flutterby (Flutterby?) dragged himself home in eighth place.

"I always want to see the best horse win the Derby," Barry wrote. "There can be no doubt that the best horse did, and Carry Back won it the way a real Derby horse should."

Barry liked the race that Carry Back ran, and he liked his trainer, too. The trainer was Jack Price, a professional horseman and amateur comedian who had some fun in Kentucky by saying, among other things, that the Derby was nothing more than the seventh race on the first Saturday in May at Churchill Downs. "Most of the things Jack Price said looked a lot worse in print," Barry wrote. "Some of the time he was just doing a little needling. On other occasions, after he'd said things half in jest, he'd be challenged. Naturally he'd stick to his guns, just as you or I would if somebody wanted to question our right to an opinion.

"I like the guy."

1964—Following Hill Rise's impressive victory in the Derby Trial, Barry wrote: "After that exhibition, only an idiot would pick against him. In this crazy world, who wants to be sane? I'm staying with Northern Dancer. This horse never runs any bad races. The only argument seems to be about how good some of his races are. I expect him to run another good race Saturday, to be out of trouble with his speed, and to win the Derby."

Northern Dancer held off Hill Rise to win that Derby in a track-record time of two minutes flat.

1967—This was the next-to-last year for the *Kentucky Irish American*, and in a column appearing the week before the Derby, Barry wrote: "Proud Clarion ran one terrible race at Hialeah when he was rushed early to get a position, but has had two fine efforts at Keeneland when allowed to come from a little off the pace. This colt obviously has class, and I'm not yet ready to dismiss him as a miler at best."

In a Derby week column, Barry provided comments on the expected starters, including:

•Dawn Glory—"There isn't a horse in Puerto Rico that can beat him. Saturday's race won't be in Puerto Rico."

•Field Master—"All the way from California at the last minute. Was this trip really necessary?"

•Diplomat Way—"I do not like Nashua horses going a mile and a quarter all in one afternoon."

•Proud Clarion—"Well bred and steadily improving, but later, baby, later."

Barry picked Damascus, the favorite. Proud Clarion, a 30–1 long shot, won.

The week after the Derby, Barry wrote: "It was 2:00³/₅ after the start when Proud Clarion finished. It was exactly 2:00⁴/₅ when the first one of my bigmouthed friends yelled in my ear, 'Later, baby, later.'

"Unfortunately, he was only the first. I figure I'll hear the last just about the time they're going in the gate May 4, 1968."

Actually, Barry *never* heard the last about not picking Proud Clarion.

Mike Barry and his wife, Bennie, in the Churchill Downs press box. (Photo by Jim Bolus)

It seems that his wife, Bennie, had been keeping up with the '67 Derby developments by reading Mike's columns and was encouraged enough by his comments on Proud Clarion to wager on the colt. In the fall of 1991, members of the media and their spouses were invited to a function in the Churchill Downs press box, and Bennie recalled that she had won a bet on the 1967 Derby based on what her husband had written about Proud Clarion.

I couldn't resist having some fun with Mike.

"Mike, if Bennie was smart enough to bet on Proud Clarion after reading what you wrote, then why didn't *you* bet on Proud Clarion?"

Good sport, that Mike Barry. He let us have our laugh.

1968—In the spring of 1967, more than eleven months before the '68 Derby, Barry covered the Bashford Manor Stakes for *The Courier-Journal & Times.*

"It's been 44 years since the Bashford Manor Stakes has produced a Kentucky Derby winner," Barry wrote, "but yesterday a lot of racing fans left Churchill Downs believing they had just seen a colt who can run for all the roses next May 4. This is T.V. Commercial, victor in the stakes race for two-year-olds after one of the most terrific stretch runs the old track has ever seen. Squeezed back to last place at the start, the son of T.V. Lark came roaring down the middle of the Downs strip to flash past Royal Exchange right at the wire. . . .

"When T.V. Commercial began to run he was a dozen lengths back, usually a fatal disadvantage in a race of only five furlongs. With [Mike] Manganello driving him hard, the Bwamazon Farm colt started picking up horses, but he was still some eight lengths back turning into the stretch. Royal Exchange, sailing along in front, appeared uncatchable, but then down the middle of the track came T.V. Commercial. An eighth of a mile from home he seemed to have no chance, at the sixteenth pole it was a faint hope,

and then just in the final yards T.V. Commercial's furious
charge carried the day."

In the next issue of the *Kentucky Irish American*, Barry
wrote: "I probably have seen more remarkable exhibi-
tions, but never one by a 2-year-old to equal the performance of T.V. Commercial in last Saturday's Bashford
Manor at Churchill Downs. Practically eliminated at the
start when the two horses on either side of him—one of
them his own stablemate—came together in front of him,
the game and handsome son of T.V. Lark still got up to
win by half a length. He gives every indication of being a
colt that will go on, besides having all the speed you could
ever want. I'm impatient to see his next start—this youngster could be something quite special."

T.V. Commercial wasn't another Man o' War, but he was
a legitimate horse, and by the end of his two-year-old season he boasted a record of six victories (including five in
stakes races), one second, and two thirds from twelve starts
with earnings of $225,739.

Barry could take pride in the fact that T.V. Commercial
made it to the 1968 Derby. The colt didn't win the Derby,
but he gave a fine account of himself in finishing fourth.
He subsequently was moved up to third after first-place
finisher Dancer's Image was disqualified from the purse
distribution.

In a column appearing in *The Louisville Times* the Monday after the Derby, Barry wrote:

"If we can get those demonstrating students out of my
office, this Little College of Thoroughbred Knowledge
will resume classes as usual. It's disgraceful, really, the
way they keep shouting they're going to stay there until I
pick a winner. Don't they ever want to see their families
again?

"During the current semester, as you know, I have
been teaching the art of expertly handicapping the Derby.

Today's lesson is part of the required course—it is absolutely essential and cannot be cut without risking expulsion. The subect: 'How to Alibi for Your Derby Loser.'"

So Barry provided alibis for these Derby horses who finished out of the money:

•Gleaming Sword, the last-place finisher ridden by Eddie Belmonte—"You know he's a come-from-behind horse. By the time Belmonte was able to get him back to last place to start his charge, the race was over."

•Verbatim—"They wouldn't let him run that mile and a quarter the way he wanted to. (He wanted to run six furlongs on Tuesday, the other four Saturday.)"

•Iron Ruler—"Baeza didn't race him right. (Braulio was too busy booting himself for getting off Dr. Fager, romping winner of the $50,000 Roseben Handicap at Aqueduct.)"

•Captain's Gig—"Ycaza could have won with him but he was afraid he'd be disqualified. (For what he would have had to do to get this horse home first, Manny would have gotten more than disqualified. Say 30 years.)"

•Te Vega—"They put him in the wrong race. (Named for a champion sailing vessel in the Pacific, Te Vega should have gone Tuesday against the Belle of Louisville and the Delta Queen.)"

•Proper Proof—"He didn't like the track. (It was a used track—most of the others had run over it before he got there.)"

•Trouble Brewing—"He's got a lot of pride—when they put him in the mutuel field it hurt his feelings."

•Don B.—"That horse showed me plenty. (Mainly what a nut anybody was to bet on him.)"

•Jig Time—"Well, he beat more than beat him. (That and $1.50 will get you a mint julep, complete with souvenir glass.)"

•Kentucky Sherry—"How did you like the way he carried them the first mile? (Don't say anything about how Combest practically had to get off and carry him the last quarter.)"

•T.V. Commercial—"You gotta admit that at 24–1 he was a playable longshot. (Joe Palmer once defined a playable longshot as a horse on which you don't get anything back, but the price is right.)"

1970—Braulio Baeza, who rode fourth-place Derby finisher Naskra, said afterward: "My horse got a little nervous before the race because of the noise and the crowd. He acted up when they started playing 'My Old Kentucky Home.'" That comment prompted Barry to write: "What a shame—we should have told the crowd to keep quiet and had the band play Brahms' Lullaby."

1972—Some of Barry's Derby Eve comments in *The Louisville Times*:

•Pacallo—"He had a good winter in Puerto Rico. Why didn't he stay there?"

•Our Trade Winds—"This one will be running at the end. The end of the day, that is."

•Napoise—"Winner of his last start at Keeneland, he could win again tomorrow—if he had the same bad horses to run against."

•Dr. Neale—"Don't say 'ah' to this Doctor. Say 'ah, never!'"

•Big Brown Bear—"I told somebody this one ought to be at the Louisville Zoo instead of the track and they said, 'But he's not a bear!' I said, 'What's the difference? He's not a race horse, either.'"

1973—In his pre-race comments, Barry wrote such gems as:

•Restless Jet—"Never underestimate the power of a woman. Also never bet on any horse owned by four women."

•Shecky Greene—"He's named for a fat comic. From the quarter pole home that's the way he'll be running."

•Gold Bag—"He won't like the track. What he won't like is all the other horses on it."

•Secretariat—"Before the Wood, he was going to make them forget Man o' War. One more race like that and nobody will remember Secretariat."

Secretariat came into the Derby off a dull third-place finish in the Wood Memorial, and Barry picked him to finish second to Sham in the Derby.

Secretariat won the Derby by 2½ lengths over Sham and set a track record of 1:59²/₅. Sham himself bettered the track record of 2:00 that Northern Dancer had set nine years earlier.

"If you're blessed with a long life," Barry wrote, "the day may come years from now when you'll say, 'Did I ever see Secretariat? Why, I was there the day he won the Derby, and let me tell you. . . .'"

Barry covered the Belmont Stakes, the race that Secretariat won by an astounding thirty-one lengths, and he led off his story in this fashion:

"It was as if they had all waited 25 years, and couldn't wait another minute. Another minute was all Secretariat needed, because he was already halfway home, but when he opened his first daylight lead on Sham the crowd of 69,138 erupted into a tremendous roar.

"They knew—all of them knew—that Secretariat was going to win the Belmont Stakes, that they were going to see the Triple Crown won. When that final minute was over, they knew something else—they had seen a great race horse. Secretariat was all of that, this big, beautiful Thoroughbred whose superiority over the others was so enormous not one of them ever got close. Not after the real race began they didn't."

And he concluded his story with this: "Secretariat has done it all. He has won the Derby, the Preakness, the Belmont, and the Triple Crown. And he has won all of his honors the way a champion should."

1974—A record number of starters—twenty-three—went to the post for this 100th Derby.

Comments by Barry included the following:

•Agitate—"Nearest the infield, so the trainer's last words to the jockey will be, 'Don't be looking for streakers—ride the race!'"

•Triple Crown—"He has a chance to start in all three of the races he's named for. He has no chance to win a single one."

•Hudson County—"Needs only a slight change in the rules, letting him run the Derby in installments. A half-mile tomorrow, another half-mile Sunday, the final quarter Monday. Or Tuesday."

•Pat McGroder—"This horse needs only one thing—slower competition. Much slower."

•Little Current—"Will be coming on at the end. So will nightfall."

Barry would produce an alibi column after the Derby, and of all the things he wrote in his career, my favorite line came when he said of twentieth-place finisher Consigliori: "Named for a character in *The Godfather*. His jockey's plan was to shoot all the other riders, but he could never get within range."

1977—Barry was a member of *The Courier-Journal & Times'* Derby ratings panel, and for some weeks leading up to the race, he thought so much of Seattle Slew that he ranked the colt 1–2–3. Realizing his mistake, Barry decided to change his ratings that appeared six days before the Derby. He made Seattle Slew 1–2–3–4–5 in his ratings.

"The official result of the Derby will be wrong," Barry wrote. "It will show horses finishing second, third, and fourth to Seattle Slew. Nonsense, of course. The nearest finisher to the winner will be so far back he'll be sixth. Maybe seventh, depending on how much Jean Cruguet lets the big horse run."

Northern Dancer, whom Barry had picked in 1964, had a son in the '77 Derby. His name was Giboulee, and Barry had this to say about him: "His trainer said he didn't like the track in the Blue Grass. Personally, I thought he loved it. Looked as if he wanted to stay on it all afternoon."

Of Sir Sir, Barry wrote: "He ran a bad race in the Flamingo. Then he ran even worse in his next start, whereupon his trainer declared him fit and ready for the Derby. Maybe a really miserable performance tomorrow will make him absolute dynamite for the Preakness."

As it turned out Sir Sir ran in all three Triple Crown races—but not very fast (twelfth in the Derby, sixth in the Preakness, and seventh in the Belmont).

All told, fourteen opponents lined up against Seattle Slew in the Derby, a development that Barry labeled beforehand as "one of the great mysteries of sport. Offhand, the smartest horseman in the country has got to be Tommy Doyle, trainer of Habitony. He's keeping his colt in California, and if Seattle Slew heads that way Tommy may take Habitony to Hawaii."

Despite a troubled trip, Seattle Slew triumphed in the Derby, and Barry would later say that this colt was "the most deserving winner" in the race's history. "In all the Derbies I've seen, I never saw a horse have as much trouble as Seattle Slew had and still win the race," he said. "He was really a good horse."

1978—This was the year of Affirmed and Calumet Farm's Alydar, and the day before the Derby, readers of *The Louisville Times* had this tip from Barry: "For the record, I'm picking Affirmed, ridden by Steve Cauthen and trained by Laz Barrera, but there's no way I could be unhappy seeing a victory for Calumet Farm and its fine young trainer, John Veitch."

Barry's 1–2–3–4 choices—Affirmed, Alydar, Believe It, and Darby Creek Road—turned out to be the exact order of finish. Barry picked the time at 2:03, which was a bit off from Affirmed's 2:01⅕. But he was the only writer to correctly pick the first four finishers, so he won *The Courier-Journal & Times'* set of six julep cups and tray.

"This ruins me," Barry said afterward. "People associate me with never being right. Now what am I going to do?"

He added: "I knew I had 'em 1–2–3–4. But I knew I was off on the time. I didn't know whether I'd win or not."

Barry explained his reasoning for his selections: "I moved Darby Creek Road up to fourth because I figured when Sensitive Prince stopped he'd stop for good. I didn't figure they'd punish him just to get a third or a fourth.

"The first three were easy. I figured Darby Creek Road was the only other good horse in the field after Sensitive Prince gave it up. You knew Sensitive Prince would go out there and battle for the lead. He can't be rated. He hasn't raced that often."

One final comment from Barry on the julep cups: "I hope they deliver them full of draft beer. I don't drink whiskey."

Barry attended the Preakness that year and watched Affirmed edge Alydar by a neck in a pulsating stretch battle. So moved by that race, he wrote: "It's amazing what a horse race can do to grown men, men who have seen thousands of races before, men who pride themselves on their ability to remain calm and observant, so that what they write later will reflect their professional judgment.

We were nothing of the sort Saturday. There I was shaking with excitement, babbling, incoherent. A turf writer of many years standing next to me said, 'I'm wound up so tight I can't breathe!' The man on the other side said, 'I was afraid my heart was gonna stop!'

"I'm almost back to normal now, at least what's normal for me. And, now that I've had a day and a half or so to think about it, there's no doubt at all. The 103rd Preakness has got to be the best race I've ever seen, because I can't think of a better one. Or a race as good, for that matter."

1979—Barry came up with these gems:

•Shamgo—"His trainer says he can run all day. That's just how much time he needs—starting late in the afternoon, he's dead."

•Sir Ivor Again—"A racetrack has been described as a place where you check your brains at the gate. If you bet on this one, be sure you don't lose your checkroom number."

•General Assembly—"The General Assembly is part of the U.N., where the Russians are always walking out. They usually walk faster than he'll be running after the first mile."

•King Celebrity—"There's something to be said for his ability, but the last time I used words like that my mother washed my mouth out with soap."

•Spectacular Bid—"The race is not to the swift, nor the battle to the strong." (Ecclesiastes 9:11) "But that's the way to bet." (Grantland Rice, 1935).

1980—Barry had this to about about the following Derby starters:

•Bold 'n Rulling—"This is one of those horses who can run all day. Unfortunately, all day won't be enough time for him to finish a mile and a quarter. You've got to be discouraged when you see his jockey leave the paddock wearing a miner's helmet and carrying sandwiches."

• Jaklin Klugman—"Owned by an actor. Once lost a photo finish because he turned his head—he wanted the camera to catch his best side."

• Hazard Duke—"He has just as much class as the 'Dukes of Hazzard' television program. If this is your favorite show, go bet a bundle on him. Anybody with your taste deserves to lose."

• Rumbo—"This is supposed to mean 'straight course' in Spanish. In English it means, 'Get a hunch and bet a bunch, and all next week you won't eat lunch.'"

• Genuine Risk—"The trainer's secret plan to win came from a telegram: 'Have her hide in the crowd at the quarter pole till they come around again, then jump in the race. Signed, Rosie Ruiz.'"

Genuine Risk won that Derby, and she did it the legal way, running the full mile and a quarter. She became the first filly since Regret in 1915 to capture the Derby.

"A few minutes after it was over," Barry wrote, "I stood up in the press box and said, 'I'll bet this is the first time a lot of you fellows ever saw a filly win the Derby.'

"Naturally there had to be a wise guy in the crowd. 'Tell me,' he said, 'did Regret win easy?'

"'Don't be ridiculous,'" I said. 'I was only five years old, and I never bet the horses seriously until I was at least seven.'"

1981—Some of Barry's pre-race comments:

• Partez—"The name is pronounced 'par-tay,' as in 'the par-tay's over.' His rider can start doing his Peggy Lee imitation on the first turn."

• Double Sonic—"A strong, brave horse with the heart of a lion. And, in the early part of the race, the speed of a water buffalo."

•Habano—"If you bet on this horse in the Derby, stay away from Mexico City. You'd go to a bullfight and bet on the bull."

•Pass the Tab—"Has never won east of the Mississippi. Unless you were lousy in geography, you know what his chances are here."

•Well Decorated—"If you like this one, try to find a ticket seller who firmly believes the South will rise again. Maybe he'll take your Confederate money."

•Classic Go Go—"This is the name he'll start with. After the first mile, they'll be calling him Classic Stop Stop."

•Television Studio—"There is something to be said for his chances, but this is a family newspaper."

Barry picked Pleasant Colony to win the Derby. He was right.

1982—Of Gato Del Sol, Barry wrote: "This means something like 'Cat of the Sun.' It also means the sun may set before he finishes."

Let's see now. The horses were off and running in the 1982 Derby at 5:40, and Gato Del Sol won the race with a time of 2:02²/₅. Sunset was at 8:34 that day . . . which means Barry miscalculated by only two hours and fifty-two minutes. So who's perfect?

1983—Barry had such observations as:

•Slew o' Gold—"Bet all the money you've got on this one—all the Confederate money, all the Monopoly money, all the Pitcairn Island money. . . ."

•Desert Wine—"Has a weight problem—the oxygen tanks his jockey must carry to get him past the quarter pole."

•Parfaitement—"In French this means 'perfectly.' In English it means you can't drag him a mile and a quarter."

1984—This was Barry's last Derby as a columnist for *The Louisville Times*, and he wrote: "How can I pick a horse that was just beaten eight big lengths by something that couldn't even qualify to run in the Derby? I threw out the race, that's all. (The sanitation men have warned that if I don't quit littering the street they'll stop picking up our garbage.) What I remember is the way Swale fought off Dr. Carter all through the stretch in the Florida Derby, and was actually pulling away at the wire. All right, so his No. 15 post position isn't good, but are there any good post positions in a field this big? I believe he has enough speed to get away in the first flight, giving [Laffit] Pincay a chance to have him well placed. This is a tough race, and Swale's a tough horse."

Naturally, Barry had fun with some of the other starters, including:

•Rexson's Hope—"Sure to be passing a lot of tired horses. Won't pass enough."

•Fali Time—"As good as anything in California. This year, that's like saying you can't find a better figure skater in Saudi Arabia."

•Raja's Shark—"The odds against being bitten by a shark in Florida are 1,000,000 to 1. In Kansas they're a lot higher. Make sure you get the Kansas odds before you buy a ticket on this one."

Barry bowed out a winner from *The Louisville Times.* Swale won the Derby by 3¼ lengths.

1990—Of Pendleton Ridge, Barry wrote: "This maiden closed well to be fourth in the Wood. No maiden has won the Derby in 57 years. After Saturday it'll be 58."

1991—Barry saw his sixty-sixth Derby in 1991.
He hadn't lost his touch.

•Green Alligator—"Supposed to have gotten his name from an Irish song. I've been to a lot of Irish parties, but no one ever reached the stage where anybody was singing about green alligators. Even if they saw some."

•Wilder Than Ever—"Has lost seven in a row. Such consistency is not a jewel."

A headline across the top of the first page of *The New Voice* told this weekly newspaper's readers all they needed to know: "Mike Barry picks Strike the Gold."

Barry wrote: "This son of Alydar has been steadily improving the last few months, he's coming to the Derby off four good races, and he'll be top weight. (Look, I know they'll all carry 126 pounds, but when he has to pick up my money . . .)"

Back in 1922, a young boy saw his first Derby and was wrong when he declared that Morvich would never last. Sixty-nine years later, Mike Barry went out a winner, picking Strike the Gold to capture the Kentucky Derby, the race that this merry gentleman loved so much.

Nick Zito, trainer of 1991 Kentucky Derby winner Strike the Gold, held The New Voice *newspaper proclaiming Mike Barry's selection.* (Photo by Billy Reed)

Sir Barton, winner of the 1919 Triple Crown. (Courtesy Keeneland-Cook)

2

Greener Pastures for Sir Barton: The First Triple Crown Winner

HOW DID A FAMOUS RACEHORSE like Sir Barton, the first Triple Crown winner, happen to be buried out on the Wyoming range, out where the deer and the antelope play?

He was born in the Bluegrass country of old Kentucky, where the best of the Thoroughbreds play.

And he won his Triple Crown, like all ten horses who won it after him, at Louisville, Baltimore, and New York.

So why bury him in a park at Douglas, Wyoming?

A statue is located over his grave at Washington Park in Douglas. In 1976, a visitor from Kentucky, wondering just how well known the Thoroughbred was to Wyomingites, asked a grizzled gas station attendant if he knew the identity of the horse buried in Washington Park. The attendant looked puzzled, then replied, "It's Man o' War. It's Man o' War, isn't it?"

At another gas station, this one located less than two furlongs from Washington Park, an attendant couldn't even venture a guess at the horse's name. "I don't know," the attendant said. "I really don't know."

Why was he honored in a town where the chamber of commerce once displayed its ignorance by referring to him as a quarter horse? And how did he become the first winner of the Triple Crown, anyway?

It all started back on April 26, 1916, when a colt was

born in a foaling barn that was to become famous as the birthplace of five Kentucky Derby winners, an old barn that still stands at Hamburg Place near Lexington, Kentucky.

John E. Madden, a brilliant horseman who was called the Wizard of the Turf, bred Sir Barton in partnership with English trainer Vivian Gooch. Madden later bought Gooch's interest in the colt and was sole owner of Sir Barton when the handsome, deep-chested chestnut began his racing career.

In his first four starts, Sir Barton failed to finish better than fifth, hardly an indication of the greatness ahead for him.

Even so, the colt had demonstrated enough promise for trainer H. Guy Bedwell, who was known around the racetrack as "Hard Guy," to buy Sir Barton at that point on behalf of J. K. L. Ross. Madden generally was reported as having sold the horse to the Ross stable for $10,000, although the price also has been listed as $9,500.

Ross, a wealthy man, was said to have inherited $12 million upon the death of his father, who helped found the Canadian Pacific Railway. Although he later would suffer financial setbacks, Ross enjoyed some big years on the racetrack. His stable ranked No. 1 in North America in money won for 1918 and 1919 and in races won in 1920, 1921, and 1922. Racing was only one interest for Ross, who also spent a lot of money on yachts and philanthropies. His full name was John Kenneth Leveson Ross. Friends called him Jack. He also was known as Commander, a title derived from his World War I command of a Royal Canadian Navy destroyer.

Bedwell, his trainer, was a highly successful horseman, but he was a tough, demanding person to work for. "Hard Guy" wasn't the only one in the stable who wouldn't have won a Mr. Congeniality contest. Neither would have Sir Barton.

The horse was an "irascible, exasperating creature" who at times was "downright evil," wrote J. K. M. Ross, son of Sir Barton's owner, in his book, *Boots and Saddles*.

". . . Sir Barton took no personal interest whatsoever in his own kind," Ross wrote, "and he complete ignored and apparently despised all human beings—with the possible exception of his groom, a huge and very dark-skinned Negro by the name of 'Toots' Thompson. Toots worshipped his charge, and I don't think he would have changed jobs with anyone."

From his sire, Star Shoot, Sir Barton inherited soft, shelly hoofs, a condition that troubled him frequently during his racing days. In running around the track, he was likely to lose a shoe and, in one race, he came back with all four missing. Shoeing was a delicate business with Sir Barton's tender feet, and Bedwell made it a practice to have a blacksmith insert a layer of piano felt between the shoe and the foot.

Bedwell used more than piano felt to prepare Sir Barton for the races.

"Sir Barton . . . is celebrated as one of the great hop-heads of history, supposed to have been coked to the eyes whenever he ran," sports columnist Red Smith once wrote. "In those days, 'touching up' was not uncommon: Ethics only forbade double-crossing form players by running an animal 'hot' one day and 'cold' the next."

Sir Barton finished his two-year-old season without a victory, but he did run second in his final race of 1918, the Futurity at Belmont Park.

Another two-year-old acquired by the Ross stable during 1918 was Billy Kelly, who lost by a head to Eternal in a match race at Laurel Park that season. The notorious gambler Arnold Rothstein reportedly won several hundred thousand dollars on that race.

Later, during the winter, Rothstein encountered Ross in a New York restaurant, and they began to compare the abilities of Billy Kelly and Eternal, who was owned by James W. McClelland.

With Rothstein favoring Eternal and Ross naturally liking his Billy Kelly, the discussion led to a sizable bet between the two men on which horse would finish ahead of the other in the Kentucky Derby. Terms of the bet specified that for either man to win, his horse had to finish in the money. (Depending on which story you believe, the bet was for either $20,000 or $50,000.)

Ross started two horses in the Derby, and the stable's contract rider, Earl Sande, had his choice of mounts— Billy Kelly, who had won sixteen of nineteen races up to then, or Sir Barton, winless in six outings and making his first start as a three-year-old. Sande, logically enough, chose Billy Kelly.

Despite his winless record, Sir Barton was accorded an excellent chance by certain observers, including Sam H. McMeekin of *The Courier-Journal.*

"The selection of the probable order of finish is wholly a matter of personal opinion," McMeekin wrote in a sports-page story that appeared on Derby Day. "The writer fancies the chances of Sir Barton. This son of Star Shoot has never won a race. But he ran second to Dunboyne in the Futurity, and in private trials this spring has demonstrated that he is a high-class colt.

"With this as the hypothesis—a band of high-class performers, one of which is receiving a twelve-pound maiden allowance—the choice must fall upon the one so benefited. A pound or two often is the margin of victory between horses of the same caliber. Twelve pounds given to a 3-year-old going the mile-and-a-quarter route in the spring is an enormous advantage. In view of the figures Sir Barton has hung up in his work this spring, twelve pounds places him at the head of the list."

Readers of this story had a Derby tip on Sir Barton, but those who noticed a front-page article in *The Courier-Journal* had to wonder whether the colt would even start. ". . . Sir Barton may not run, it is said," the paper stated without elaborating.

Johnny Loftus, an accomplished jockey who had won the 1916 Derby with George Smith, was named to ride Sir Barton. With Loftus unable to make the weight of 110, Sir Barton went to the post carrying 112½ pounds.

Sir Barton was sent out to accomplish one primary mission. The game plan for the Ross horses was for Sir Barton to set a fast early pace in the hope that he would burn out Eternal and set it up for Billy Kelly to make his move in the stretch. It didn't exactly work out that way.

At the outset, Sir Barton was doing his part, leading by two lengths the first time past the stands, while arch-rivals Eternal and Billy Kelly were running second and third. At the far turn Billy Kelly rushed up to take over second, and when the field hit the top of the stretch, Eternal was dropping farther and farther back, a thoroughly whipped horse.

By now, it was obvious that Billy Kelly would beat Eternal. Sir Barton was expected to tire out and relinquish the lead to his stablemate. Trouble was, Sir Barton wasn't ready to conk out. Furthermore, Loftus was having trouble spotting Billy Kelly. At least, that's what he said afterward.

"I stood up in the stirrups and looked around to see where Sande and Billy Kelly were," said Loftus, who shouldn't really have had to look too hard, or too far, to spot them. Sande and Billy Kelly were right behind him, not more than a length and a half back, but Loftus said he couldn't see them.

Loftus thought, "What a shame. If this little horse had been rated and saved, he would have come back the winner."

Funny thing. Loftus then quit looking for Sande and Billy Kelly and proceeded to look for one thing—the finish line. "Seeing nothing of Billy Kelly, I gave Sir Barton a cut of the whip, and he jumped off as if it were the start. Then I rode him the rest of the way, figuring to hell with Bedwell, Sande, and Billy Kelly . . . ," he recalled.

After Billy Kelly closed the gap some nearing the three-sixteenths pole, Sir Barton drew away to achieve the first victory of his career. Billy Kelly finished five lengths back in second place, marking the first time that the same stable ran one-two in the Derby. The highly regarded Eternal, disdaining the heavy going, dragged himself home tenth.

Ross had a profitable day. Sir Barton earned $20,825 for winning the Derby, and Billy Kelly picked up $2,500 for second. Furthermore, in a few days, Ross received a check from Mr. Rothstein, a controversial man whose name would be mentioned later in connection with the Black Sox baseball scandal of 1919 and who would be murdered in a 1928 New York shooting.

Sir Barton didn't have much time to rest after the Derby. It was on by rail to Baltimore, where the Preakness was held just four days after the Derby. Sir Barton carried 126 pounds in the Preakness, the same impost packed by Eternal, who had spotted the Ross colt $9\frac{1}{2}$ pounds in the Derby.

Sir Barton, sent off as the favorite with stablemate Milkmaid, won the Preakness by four lengths over runner-up Eternal. Ten days later, Sir Barton was back in action, and he won the Withers.

His next start was the Belmont, a race in which he had only two opponents, and he won by five lengths with ease. His time for the Belmont, then a mile and three-eighths, was $2:17\frac{2}{5}$, an American record for that distance.

In a month's time, Sir Barton had come a long way. From a maiden, he had won four important races for three-year-olds, including the Kentucky Derby, the Preakness, and the Belmont—three events that later would be recognized as racing's Triple Crown.

That brings us back to the Sir Barton statue that now stands in tree-studded Washington Park in Douglas, Wyoming. In a pamphlet listing all the sights and sounds of the town, the Douglas Chamber of Commerce once referred to Sir Barton as the first quarter-horse Triple Crown winner.

"That was the dumbest thing I heard of," recalled Gordon Turner, the Douglas man who led a drive that moved Sir Barton's remains in 1968 from a run-down spot outside the town to Washington Park.

"I raised hell over that," Turner said. The chamber didn't make that mistake again.

Sir Barton stood in Wyoming for the last four years of his life. He raced for three seasons (1918–20) before Ross sold him early in his stud career to B. B. and Montfort Jones, brothers who owned Audley Farm in Virginia. Sir Barton stayed at the Berryville, Virginia, farm for several years before being "farmed out" in Kentucky.

"Sir Barton was advertised to stand at Audley in the spring of 1922 at a fee of $500 with no return," reported *The Blood-Horse*. "For the next three seasons he stood at $1,000 with no return. After that Audley Farm ceased to advertise him, and though his get won more than $100,000 for three consecutive years (1928–30), the tradition was now being fixed in the minds of breeders that no son of Star Shoot could be a success as a sire. Sir Barton gradually was accepted as a failure. . . ."

Sir Barton wasn't a total failure at stud, however. He did sire eight stakes winners, including Easter Stockings, who earned $91,435 and won the 1928 Kentucky Oaks.

Still, he did not set the world on fire at stud, and in 1933 he was turned over to the Remount Division of the U.S. Army. He ended up at a remount station at Ft. Robinson, Nebraska. His stud fee was reported to be between five and ten dollars. Later in the year, the Remount Division placed him at Dr. J. R. Hylton's ranch in the foothills of the Laramie Mountains, not far from Douglas.

The twenty-one-year-old horse died October 30, 1937, from an attack of acute intestinal colic. In a telegram to *The Blood-Horse* magazine, Dr. Hylton said Sir Barton was very vigorous and in good flesh and "looked considerably less than his age" but that he had suffered several attacks of colic in the previous year.

Sir Barton was buried on the range near the Wagon Hound Creek, and a sandstone marker was placed over the grave.

In time, Dr. Hylton died, ownership of the ranch changed, and the grave site deteriorated. "When Sir Barton died," Turner said, "Dr. Hylton had a little wooden fence around the grave, and it didn't look too bad. But then, of course, the farm changed hands, and the grave just had gone to pot out there. I didn't think he belonged out there anymore. I just thought it was too bad for him. That's why I thought he should be located here in Douglas."

A letter from Turner appeared in *The Thoroughbred Record*, a now-defunct weekly magazine, asking for contributions that would go toward a statue over Sir Barton's new grave. He also wrote some prominent horse people for contributions, but he received virtually no assistance from them, except for a grandson of John E. Madden, Lexington's Preston Madden, co-owner of Hamburg Place with his brother, Patrick. Preston Madden donated a plaque, which was placed at the base of the statue.

Two other persons who didn't forget Sir Barton were his old grooms, each of whom made a small, but sincere, contribution.

Turner remembered well the letter he received from the man who groomed Sir Barton during his racing career.

"His letter was a classic," Turner said. "The English wasn't very good, or the spelling, but you could make it out. I figured he must have been in his 80s or 90s. And he wanted to send a dollar. I thought that meant a lot to him, that dollar. I was sure that meant more to him on a fixed income than anyone else that donated."

The other groom was Tom Morgan, who took care of Sir Barton during his retirement days at Audley Farm. "He was one of the ruffest [sic] studs I ever handled," Morgan wrote Turner. ". . . I want to thank you for what you're doing for the sake of the old horse, and in the remembrance of him I gladly send this."

Lacking support from racing people, Turner turned to the Douglas Junior Chamber of Commerce, which went about the business of raising the money for the statue. It cost about $2,000.

In his book, *The Most Glorious Crown,* author Marvin Drager wrote of the statue: "It appears that the heroic statue is not a likeness of Sir Barton. Rather, it is a fiberglass replica of 'a' horse. . . ."

Turner didn't appreciate that.

"I was real disappointed with the way that was written," he said. "We are real sorry it wasn't a bronze statue in Sir Barton's image, but we didn't have the money. This is a fiberglass statue done in bronze color. I think it looks quite nice myself."

The paint was chipped off the statue slightly in places. Names and initials were scratched on it, and splotches of white paint were daubed on the eyes. "It's a shame people couldn't have left it alone," Turner said in 1976.

However, in a recent interview, Turner said that the statue was reburbished in 1992. "It looks pretty good now," he said in 1993.

Turner attended Transylvania College in Lexington, Kentucky, for a semester in 1952. "I went to college back there just strictly so I could go to the farms and stuff," Turner said.

"I didn't care about the education part," he added. "I had my classes set up so I was off at noon every day. And I visited the farms and went to Keeneland when they were open in the afternoon."

Turner, a native of Douglas, was just three years old when Sir Barton died in 1937 so his knowledge of the horse stemmed from what he has read and heard.

Not so with Bob Moore, a veteran rancher who remembered Sir Barton standing in Wyoming.

"I think he was a helluva good horse—very good," Moore said. "He was just the kind of horse that everbody in this part of the country really wanted. He was a Thoroughbred on the quarter-horse type. By that, I mean he wasn't a great big, leggy, long-legged Thoroughbred. He was a heavy-muscled Thoroughbred horse. More like the horses that we like to ride, really."

According to one story that has circulated in Wyoming, the horse that Roy Rogers owned and used in his last movies was a grandson of Sir Barton. But a check with Rogers' office disclosed that the cowboy star had no knowledge of Sir Barton.

Sir Barton obviously isn't a household word out in cowboy country. But back in 1919 he earned a niche in sports history by becoming the first horse to win racing's Triple Crown.

Thoroughbred racing's, that is.

3

Judge Daingerfield
Set the Standard

During Keene Daingerfield's distinguished career as a racing official, one axiom always held true: When he spoke, people listened.

The former steward from Kentucky commanded so much respect that his word traditionally was considered the gospel. Indeed, it is no exaggeration to say that he may very well have been the most respected official in the history of American racing.

When Daingerfield received the prestigious 1985 Eclipse Award of Merit, one account stated that during his career he "came to represent all that was right with Thoroughbred racing. The wealth of knowledge he developed during his career as a trainer provided an excellent background for the stewards' stands. He proved to be healthily suspicious and came to be regarded as shrewd, fair, and meticulous in his dealings, a role model for his colleagues, and an accessible figure to all licensees under his jurisdiction."

As knowledgeable and erudite as Daingerfield was, he was more than a good talker. He was a good listener, too—a trait that helped him enormously in his career. Around the racetrack, everybody knew one thing: You could talk to Mr. Daingerfield.

It should be noted that after Daingerfield listened, he didn't always reply in such a fashion that pleased the talker, but at least he heard a person's complaint, he was interested in what he or she had to say, and, most of all, he cared.

The esteemed Keene Daingerfield served as steward at thirteen runnings of the Kentucky Derby (1974–86). Each year the Keene Daingerfield Award is presented at the Derby Trainers Dinner, which is held by the Kentucky Thoroughbred Owners and Breeders on Tuesday of Derby Week in Louisville. The Keene Daingerfield Award was established by the Kentucky State Racing Commission in recognition of Daingerfield's lifelong dedication to the Thoroughbred racing industry. The award is given to an individual whose contributions and accomplishments have resulted in the betterment of the Thoroughbred racing industry. In 1983, Daingerfield was the first recipient of this award. (Courtesy Keeneland Association)

As his longtime colleague Jack Goode once put it, "He loved it, and he worked hard at it 365 days a year. He was the most knowledgeable, he was well-educated, and he grew up in it from training horses."

Tom Meeker, the Churchill Downs president since 1984, speaks in glowing terms of Daingerfield's career as a steward. "I came to the track in the twilight really of Keene's career," Meeker said, "but it became readily obvious that there was something unique and special about Keene. I think the first thing you recognized was that he was a gentleman in the truest sense. No. 2, he had an absolute love for horse racing. And No. 3, he packed as much integrity as any human being I've ever seen; and I saw that displayed in a number of situations—in the stand, at commission meetings, and in dealing with people one on one. He was a *wonderful* man."

Bernie Hettel, who succeeded Daingerfield as Kentucky state steward, is thankful for the time that he spent learning from the veteran racing official. "He really set the standard by which all stewards and racing officials are measured," Hettel said. "He certainly did that by his exuberance for the position and his intellect. He was my mentor. It made it easier on me by knowing exactly how the job was to be performed by simply observing him for several years before I got in the stand. I had the extreme pleasure of being side by side with him for about a year and a half, two years before he actually retired from one spot, and then he stayed on as an association [racetrack] steward. Of course, that was an immense help in a transition period. He never really let me fall on my face."

Jerry Botts, the racing secretary at Churchill Downs since the fall of 1984, began working at that track as an official in the spring of 1973, and late that summer Daingerfield came on board as state steward in Kentucky. Botts fondly recalls his experiences with Daingerfield, saying: "He was one of the most intelligent men I believe I ever was around, as far as making intelligent decisions on things that would come up during a race. He had a knack for doing a logical thing that made some sense to solve a problem. He was very wise. He had a wisdom kind of like Solomon. After he would rule on something or make a decision, and then when you would think about it, you'd say, 'Well, that's so obvious. Why didn't I think about it?' He would help you, he would get with you, he would explain things to you. He was one of those people that you weren't intimidated by, because it was always easy to ask him questions."

Daingerfield, who was elected to The Jockey Club in 1989, brought honor and integrity and dedication to the stewards' stand. Not only was he known as an all-around horse person, he was recognized for his versatility in other fields. To be sure, he was a gifted writer, one who could turn a phrase and demonstrate a sense of humor with the pen. In 1942, he wrote a book entitled *Training for Fun, and Profit—Maybe!* His dedication read: "To My Aunt ELIZABETH DAINGERFIELD—who thinks all trainers are butchers."

In his preface, he wrote: "The writer trembles at undertaking this book, lest its purpose be misunderstood. The text is not about how to train a horse, but simply about training horses, and I hope the distinction is clear. . . . The primary thing for the neophyte to remember is that there is no legerdemain connected with training horses, no sleight of hand, no magic words to change a bad horse into a good one. . . . The trainer who gets maximum results from average material is the good trainer. Luck, too, plays a prominent part; but luck, as a substitute for brains, does not last forever."

With a flair and a way with words, Daingerfield no doubt could have been a successful writer, but he was destined for the stewards' stand, not the press box.

Even so, he relied on his writing ability as a steward. In

the early 1970s, he collaborated with *The Blood-Horse* magazine's Kent Hollingsworth on a racing rulebook. After returning to Kentucky in 1973, he rewrote a rulebook the following year, with a great deal of legal assistance from Louisville attorney Edward S. ("Ned") Bonnie. Most of the rules that he could claim any general adoption for were written by him in either New Jersey or Florida.

J. Keene Daingerfield, Jr., had roots in the horse business. Born on December 12, 1910, in Lexington, Kentucky, he was the grandson of Foxhall A. Daingerfield, who managed brother-in-law James R. Keene's highly successful Castleton Farm.

An uncle, Algernon Daingerfield, served as secretary of The Jockey Club in New York for many years, and an aunt, Elizabeth Daingerfield, was one of the most knowledgeable people—man or woman—in the horse industry during the early part of this century. Lizzie (or Miss Lizzie), as Daingerfield referred to her, was a well-known pedigree expert and was instrumental in getting the legendary Man o' War's stud career launched upon his retirement from racing following the 1920 season.

"Lizzie was essentially ladylike—but pretty damn tough," Daingerfield recalled. For years, she carried a holstered Derringer on her hip, although Daingerfield noted, "She never shot anybody."

Daingerfield saw his first Kentucky Derby in 1924 at the age of thirteen. His father, Keene, Sr., was a horse lover and a lawyer. Daingerfield himself attended the University of Virginia for almost three years to pursue a legal education. But he returned home after his mother died, and in 1933 he took out his trainer's license. After working as an owner and trainer, he served in the military for 2½ years during World War II.

"I served with the Army engineers, a placement I find mystifying to this day," Daingerfield recalled in a 1983 interview. "Up until that time, I'd never used a tool more complicated than a pitchfork, and the only machine I understood was a sled."

Daingerfield trained horses for about fifteen years, conditioning among others George Gains, who captured the 1948 Churchill Downs Handicap. "Frankly, I was just beginning to find out what it was all about when I quit," he once said. "I never really had much material to work with, and I was actually conceited enough to think I did fairly well with inferior material. I came to the point where I realized that Ben Jones would know in six minutes what it took me six weeks to find out.

"You've got to know a horse's hole card. Every horse has a peculiarity, some quality that will enable you to get the best out of that animal. Given time enough, I could discover those hole cards, but I decided to my own satisfaction that I couldn't recognize these conditions as quickly as a top trainer would. I thought I could be a top racing official, rather doubted that I would become a top trainer."

So in 1948, Daingerfield launched his career as a racing official, taking a job as steward at Narragansett Park in Rhode Island. The following year he was named secretary of the Kentucky State Racing Commission.

He was state steward in Illinois from 1953 to 1956 and in New Jersey from 1966 to 1973. He returned to Kentucky in 1973 at a time when this state's racing industry, which was suffering through some controversial times, was crying out for a steadying hand.

"We think that with all the turmoil and trouble we've had in racing, here as in other places, he will be a leveling influence," Kentucky State Racing Commission chairman William H. May said in announcing Daingerfield's appointment as senior steward and chief administrator for the commission.

Despite the huge black eye that Kentucky racing had received during those troublesome times, something good resulted from the situation. That something was the hiring of Keene Daingerfield. His return to Kentucky was applauded by those who knew that a change was needed and that he was the perfect man for the job.

"I learned long ago that revolutionizing racing is a hazardous business," Daingerfield said at the time. "I don't believe in revolutionizing racing, and I don't see myself as a new broom or anything of that sort."

In his own way, Daingerfield went about the business of helping Kentucky racing overcome its problems. Daingerfield served as state steward in Kentucky for 12½ years before resigning from that position in February 1985, although he continued to work on occasion at Keeneland and Churchill Downs for the next several years.

After Daingerfield was named recipient of the '85 Eclipse Award of Merit, Timothy T. Capps wrote in *The Thoroughbred Record*: "He is an honored and honorable member of his profession, retired now at 75, but hopefully a point of reference in future years for those who care about the soul of this sport. For a prototype of the consummate racing official, look no further than Keene Daingerfield, gentleman of the Old South, Eclipse Award winner of 1985. They must be cheering in Stewards Heaven."

All told, he was a steward at 20 tracks in 11 states for 40 years.

This Southern gentleman served in the stewards' stand for the Derbies of 1974–86. Before 1974, he had officiated at thousands of horse races, including many $100,000-plus stakes, but not until that year did he work in the stewards' stand for a Derby. "Frankly, I was scared to death," he recalled with a chuckle.

"As far as procedure is concerned, it's just another horse race," he added in a 1975 interview. "On the other hand, I'd be lying to you if I said I regarded it as just another horse race. As far as watching the race, certainly you are not going to let your attention flag for an instant.

"Of course, you shouldn't let your attention flag for the ninth race on Tuesday, but we'll just say human nature being what it is, you're more alert, more on your toes for any stakes race. That doesn't mean that you consciously let down for minor races, but certainly for the Derby—or for *any* stake—you watch the [post] parade more closely, you have the colors in mind. If post positions differ from the program numbers, you're probably more aware that No. 2 is breaking from stall No. 14, or things of that sort."

Writing in the *1987 Kentucky Derby Souvenir Magazine*, Daingerfield had this to say about the Churchill Downs classic: "The Kentucky Derby is not 'just another horse race,' and anyone who says it is doesn't know what he's talking about or doesn't give a damn about racing. 'Derby fever' sets in about two weeks before the race and becomes increasingly nerve-wracking until the 'official' sign is posted. Derby Week is great fun, but it's also a grave responsibility. After all, Breeders' Cup to the contrary, this is still the great showcase for American racing. We— the stewards—are acutely aware of this. We do, however, make a sincere effort to 'judge' the race exactly as we would the last race on a Tuesday; but don't expect any snap judgments or quick decisions. If we're wrong, we're a long time wrong."

Of the thirteen Derbies he officiated from the stewards' stand, Daingerfield said "the performance of Angel Cordero, Jr., on Bold Forbes in 1976 stands out. Angel seized the initiative at the break, cut out his own running, and nursed and coaxed a game horse beyond his physical parameters to actually increase his lead in the last 100 yards. He also permitted his mount, under a left-hand whip, to drift out exactly as far as was permissible, and not an inch farther. I don't think he could have heard us yelling, 'Take ahold of him, Angel,' but he did it anyhow."

In 1983 and 1984, before he took over as state steward, Hettel accompanied Daingerfield to the jockeys' room before the Derby and listened to the veteran judge talk to the riders. "He tried to calm everybody and welcome them," Hettel said.

Hettel recalled that Daingerfield would deliver the following message to the jockeys: "Just because the media thinks there'll never be a disqualified Kentucky Derby winner on a riding infraction, don't think that's true. I'll take a number down—and don't think I won't. Don't become famous for being the guy who had your number taken down in the Kentucky Derby. You'll make the history book, but it'll be that disgrace of having won the Kentucky Derby, only to be disqualified."

In 1984, Daingerfield was in the stand for the first disqualification of a Derby starter as a result of an incident that occurred in the race. Gate Dancer finished fourth but was disqualified to fifth for lugging in and bumping Fali Time several times in the homestretch.

There were other incidents in the Derby during Daingerfield's tenure in the stewards' stand.

In 1975, Derby runner-up Avatar and third-place finisher Diabolo were involved in a bumping match in the homestretch. Immediately afterward, the stewards posted an inquiry to view the patrol film of the incident. After studying the patrol film, Daingerfield and colleagues Jack Goode and Leo O'Donnell decided that Diabolo was responsible for starting the trouble.

"We felt that if Diabolo had not lurched into Avatar and turned him out, nothing would have happened," Daingerfield said. "The horse that suffered most was Diabolo, but I think it's pretty obvious that this did not affect the actual result of the race."

Years later, Daingerfield recalled a sidelight of the 1975 Derby in this fashion: "I had been 'schooled' all week with the procedure to be followed with television in the event that there was an inquiry or objection. A direct telephone line had been installed between the stewards' and presentation stands. In case anything happened, I was supposed to pick up this phone and explain to Howard Cosell, who would answer it, what was going on. As soon as the inquiry sign went up, Jack or Leo gave the required information to the track announcer, and I picked up the hot line.

"'Mr. Cosell' . . . no answer. 'Mr. Cosell' [louder] . . . still no answer. 'HOWARD' [screaming]. He hasn't answered yet, and I never knew what, if anything, he said."

In 1977, Seattle Slew got off to a nearly disastrous start, coming out of the gate from his No. 4 post position and veering to his right somewhat. The race had just begun, and already this heavy favorite was last. Asked to run in a hurry by jockey Jean Cruguet in order to get back into the race, Seattle Slew forced his way through the field. After passing the eighth pole the first time, the charging Seattle Slew came out and bumped Bob's Dusty. "I didn't think it was a major incident," Daingerfield said soon after the race. "But there is no doubt that he did come out off For The Moment's heels and hit Bob's Dusty a pretty good bump. If Bob's Dusty had finished where Run Dusty Run did, we probably would have had some trouble."

As it was, there was no trouble. Bob's Dusty finished far back in eleventh place, while his entrymate, Run Dusty Run, ran second to Seattle Slew. "I think it would have been ridiculous to disqualify Seattle Slew for bumping a horse that finished quite far back at a point where there were still nine furlongs to go," Daingerfield logically explained.

Daingerfield labeled 1948 Triple Crown champion Citation "the best horse I ever saw in action."

When it came to the best trainer and jockey he ever saw, he named two Hall of Famers—Ben. A. Jones and Eddie Arcaro.

Of Arcaro, Daingerfield said: "First, he was strong. Second, he was fearless. Third, he had an absolute economy of action; every muscle was in perfect tune with the animal."

Daingerfield called the 1988 Breeders' Cup Distaff at Churchill Downs "the greatest race I ever saw." That was the race that Personal Ensign won in the last jump over Kentucky Derby winner Winning Colors, thus completing her career with an unbeaten record.

Daingerfield saw many memorable races, met many well-known people, made many important decisions during his lifetime. He could have written a book on his experiences, especially those in the stewards' stand.

Some of his comments about the job of a steward:

"A steward's duty is to interpret and enforce the rules of racing. The stewards are the first and foremost line of defense against improper practices, and stewards can exercise at least nominal control over the other racing officials. Stewards do, to this extent, run the whole show. It's not too often we have an opportunity to do something sensational, to uncover a putative jockey ring or such. Very rarely do we do anything sensational. Rather, we set the tone for the meeting.

"It is hard for the public to realize that we can't deal in personalities, that we only deal in black and white. Stewards don't spring from cabbage leaves. All stewards have friends, past associations, some enemies, past experiences—but you try to put these things out of your mind. You try to avoid being close friends with people in the business.

"My philosophy is that if there's any doubt in my mind, I would prefer to leave the number up. In other words, you're not looking for reasons to disqualify a horse.

"I'd have to say the increase in litigation faced by racing officials is the main change for the worse I've seen since I became a steward. There are so many things that people can sue you over these days."

Looking back on his career as a steward, Daingerfield once said: "It can be the source of a lot of satisfaction when you know you've done the right thing. It is especially gratifying when you explain to someone who has violated a rule just how he's done so and he accepts it."

In 1965, Daingerfield wrote an article suggesting that an aspiring steward be "equipped with the qualities of integrity, courage, judgment, experience, patience, and a good memory."

As an afterthought, he added, "Plus the hide of a rhinoceros."

Daingerfield, who died September 1, 1993, at the age of eighty-two, influenced and assisted many people during his lengthy career in racing. Dave Hooper, coordinator of the University of Arizona Race Track Industry Program, knows full well the many contributions that Daingerfield made to racing.

"In the spring of 1976, I had the good fortune to be offered the opportunity to join the Kentucky State Racing Commission as associate state steward and work under the supervision and tutelage of Keene Daingerfield," Hooper recalled. "Having had longtime aspirations to become a steward, I couldn't conceive of a better scenario than to be able to be at the right hand of the recogized dean of American racing officials and learn the steward's role and responsibilities. Shortly after the 1976 Kentucky Derby, I became the fourth member of the Churchill Downs stewards' stand, sitting as an observer for several weeks in the company of Keene, Jack Goode, and Leo O'Donnell."

Hooper noted that those three men collectively represented more than 100 years of experience as stewards.

"I learned from them the importance of communication within a board of stewards, diplomacy, tact, sharing of responsibilities, handling administrative matters, dealing with commissioners, race-watching from an official's perspective, film [videotape] analysis, and preventive medicine, i.e., taking action to prevent an untoward incident from happening before it has a chance to happen.

"Because stewards are required to make numerous decisions in the course of any working day—some related to licensing and application of rules while in the stewards' office and others related to incidents occurring in the course of a race that are decided in the stewards' stand—they are frequently hailed as 'judge.' When licensees visited with Keene and addressed him as 'judge,' it was always in a tone of respect bordering on reverence. Daingerfield's presence at any racetrack or racing meeting was accompanied by an air of authority unmatched in other jurisdictions and a firm confidence that the regulation of each racing day was in good hands.

"Daingerfield had a reputation for being able to give a licensee the bad news about an impending suspension in words and in a way that would cause the licensee to leave the stewards' office smiling—and just before leaving often turn around and say, 'Thank you, Judge.'

"He was in the forefront among officials as a leader and innovator. At one time, he headed the now-defunct officials' organization known as SNARO—the Society of North American Racing Officials. Officials in many jurisdictions frequently sought his counsel and guidance on matters they had before them. Daingerfield would willingly share his expertise and advice with colleagues and teach and encourage less-experienced officials.

"Daingerfield was a longtime proponent of racing experience in the stewards' stand. He considered it an affront to qualified stewards to be paired in the stand with a political appointee whose sole qualification for the position was the result of political favoritism and financial support of a governor. He would be pleased that those days appear to be ending.

"His skilled and prolific writings, including 'Qualifications and Standards for a Racing Steward' published by the Association of Racing Commissioners International, have been incorporated into the resource books utilized in

Keene Daingerfield. (Photo by Bill Straus, courtesy Keeneland Association)

the Racing Laws and Enforcement classes which I teach as part of the University of Arizona Race Track Industry Program curriculum.

"In addition, those same writings, as well as many Daingerfield actions and decisions, are shared with participants in racing officials seminars conducted by both the University of Arizona Race Track Industry Program and the University of Lousiville Equine Administration Department.

"Through the conduct of racing official seminars and offering of regulatory classes within two university programs, the Keene Daingerfield contributions to good officiating are being preached over and over again—and his legacy lives on."

Owner Fred Hooper led Hoop Jr. to the winner's circle following the 1945 Kentucky Derby. Trainer Ivan Parke walked alongside Hooper, and Eddie Arcaro was up on Hoop Jr. (Courtesy Keeneland-Morgan)

4

"I Never Thought I'd Make It This Quick"

BACK IN 1945, after winning the Kentucky Derby with Hoop Jr., the very first Thoroughbred he ever purchased, Fred Hooper said, "I never thought I'd make it this quick."

Words to remember, those.

Eddie Arcaro, who rode Hoop Jr. to his Derby victory, also spoke some words worth remembering. "That's the most expensive race you'll ever win," he told Hooper after the Derby.

"Why?" wondered Hooper.

"You'll spend the rest of your life trying to win it again."

Hooper has done just that.

Now, almost half a century later, Hooper is still trying to win his second Derby.

Hooper has failed with three subsequent Derby starters—Olympia, sixth in 1949; Crozier, second in 1961; and Admiral's Voyage, ninth in 1962. All three of those colts were in contention in the homestretch of their Derby bids. The pacemaking Olympia led by a length after a mile, Crozier held a half-length lead at the stretch call and wasn't overtaken by Carry Back until inside the sixteenth pole, and Admiral's Voyage was battling for the lead with a quarter of a mile to go before tiring.

Hooper seemed to have an excellent chance to reach the race in 1982 with at least one of two colts, Journey at Sea or Advance Man. "I would like to see both horses in the winner's circle—as a dead heat," he said slightly more than a month before that Derby. But, alas, Journey at Sea didn't get to the Kentucky Derby after being pressed hard to do so, and Advance Man was injured in the Arkansas Derby.

In 1983, Hooper had hopes of running Copelan for the roses. Copelan opened the year as the Derby's future-book favorite but was forced to miss the race after being hurt in the Blue Grass Stakes at Keeneland Race Course.

Winning the Derby is a difficult assignment for any three-year-old. Just getting to the race also can be a tough task, as evidenced by Copelan's misfortune in the Blue Grass. After the race, Hooper was particularly critical of Marfa's antics, blaming that horse for causing most of the trouble. Later, Hooper said of Copelan's effort in the Blue Grass: "He was running very good, and the outside horse [Marfa] came in on him and the inside horse [the victorious Play Fellow] came out and put him in a squeeze. The jockey tried to stop him from running, and it strained muscles in his back. He also got hit on his right foreleg. This accident was something like you driving your car at 70 miles per hour and someone pulled out in front of you and you would put all the pressure you could on your brakes. You would put a big strain on your car. This is what happened to Copelan."

Hooper also had a candidate for the 1984 Derby, a speedy colt by the name of Precisionist. But Precisionist didn't win the Santa Anita Derby, the race he had to win in order for Hooper to put him on a plane to Kentucky. Precisionist finished second as the favorite, and Hooper decided to keep him in California.

"I thought if the colt could win the race out there that we'd come on with him to the Derby," Hooper said at the time. "He run a big race, but I just figured to ship him in to Kentucky for the Derby and then bring him back to California and all, it was just too much for him.

"I'm not interested in just going to the Derby and running a horse. Some people seem to not care just as long as they get a horse to run in the Derby. Precisionist is a free-running horse and just loves to go out and run. I figured there's a lot of time yet for him to run in a lot of races."

As it turned out, Precisionist became the first horse to run in four renewals of the Breeders' Cup championship card. He finished seventh in the 1984 Classic; first in the 1985 Sprint; third in the 1986 Classic; and after experiencing a fertility problem at stud, returned to action in 1988 and ran fifth in the Sprint that year.

Hooper, who turned ninety-six in 1993, has never lost his enthusiasm for racing and for life. For years, he kept a pace that would have left many much younger men worn out. Friends were amazed by his stamina and durability. After staying at a party well into the night, he was known to be the first person to show up at the barn the next morning, looking fresher than ever. An early riser, Hooper traveled frequently and liked to stay on the go. Hooper has remained active even in his mid-nineties, although he doesn't maintain the pace that he once did.

Tireless in his efforts to help the racing industry, Hooper has left his mark on the sport in many ways. He was one of the first owners to use air transportation for horses, and he was among the original Easterners to race in California. He provided outstanding leadership in Florida, and he was instrumental in the development of housing facilities for females at certain racetracks.

Moreover, in a sport that has become more and more a game of partnerships and syndications, Hooper has maintained his independence. With very few exceptions in the operation of his Thoroughbred business, he's owned 100 percent of every one of his horses.

"I just feel like that what I have I want to own myself," he explained. "I just have always felt like that whatever I do, if it's wrong, why then I'll be to blame. I was in heavy construction, building roads and airports and dams over six of the southeastern states for 36 years, and I just didn't want a partner, that's all."

Hooper also had an impact on racing by giving three jockeys who went on to greatness—Braulio Baeza, Laffit Pincay, Jr., and Jorge Velasquez—their start in the United States.

Pincay began riding in the United States in 1966. "I'm very grateful to Mr. Hooper because he gave me the opportunity to come to this country and ride for him," Pincay said. "He put me on some nice horses at the beginning of my career, and I won some good races for him."

With a laugh, Pincay added, "I remember he used to tease me a lot. He used to come by in the morning while I was working horses and he would come beside me and pull some change out of his pocket and he would say to me, 'Listen, I'm kinda broke so you better start winning some races so I can fill up my pocket.'"

Velasquez was Hooper's contract jockey for three years.

"Mr. Hooper was the one who opened up the door for me in this country," Velasquez said. "He was wonderful to me for three years. He's a wonderful person, and he's a man of his word."

And he's a man who's sincerely devoted to his horses and to racing.

"I have never known anyone like Fred Hooper," said Chuck Tilley, who was executive director of the Florida Thoroughbred Breeders' Association during the years (1971–79) that Hooper served as the group's president. "I'm extremely fortunate that I've been able to know him and spend some time with him. You don't find another one like him."

Tilley and his late wife, Bette, knew Hooper for years, and both said they had never heard him raise his voice. But when Hooper speaks, he gets his message across, to be sure. During his progressive administration with the

FTBA, legislators in Florida paid close attention to what Hooper had to say.

"I worked at it, and we got things passed in Tallahassee that nobody had gotten passed before," said Hooper.

Very few people today in the racing industry—not just in the United States but throughout the world—are held in such high esteem as Fred Hooper. And what's most admirable about this man is that he's gained his stature in the sport by doing things one way and one way only. His way.

"Hooper is his own man—always has been," Hall-of-Fame trainer and former Tartan Farms president Johnny Nerud once said. "He hears a different tune. He listens to the beat of Fred Hooper. That's the only beat he listens to. But it works out pretty good. Hooper is an excellent leader, he's an excellent executive, and he's an extremely good horse breeder."

When Tartan began its Ocala operation years ago, Nerud knew whose breeding methods to observe. "I watched Hooper extremely carefully because I think he is one of the best breeders we've ever had in the business," Nerud said. "He breeds them the way Hooper sees them, he does not spend the big money and he comes up with winner after winner after winner for year after year after year, so he's a man you could study very carefully and not go wrong."

Generally breeding his own mares to his own stallions, he in effect developed his own "Hooper line." Along the way, he has received an Eclipse Award twice as the country's top breeder, in 1975 and 1982. He also was honored with the 1991 Eclipse Award of Merit.

Hooper has been around a long time, and it's only natural to refer to him as the Grand Old Man of Racing. In 1984, Nerud disagreed with that reference, saying: "Hooper never got old. He thinks young. He still wants to win, and he wants to go and he wants to be there—and he's not old."

Fred Hooper, this Grand Young Man of Racing, will never be one to sit back in a rocking chair and watch life go by, but in 1984 this gentleman did cross his legs and lean back in a chair in his home in Ocala and talk about his life and philosophies, about his horses and Hooper Academy, and about his bets and his buddies.

Soft-spoken and down-to-earth, Hooper had a good sense of humor and excellent recall of the events in his life.

His roots trace to Cleveland, Georgia, where he was born October 6, 1897, on his father's farm. He was one of ten children.

Fred William Hooper, a man who believes in himself, made his reputation as the head of Hooper Construction Company and as the owner of his vast racing stable, but he has tried his hand at a number of other jobs in his lifetime. The industrious Hooper worked as a timber cutter and carpenter, as a barber and steel worker. In addition, he grew potatoes and raised cattle. He also tried both hands at something else—boxing—and during his younger days in Muscle Shoals, Alabama, he was the town's heavyweight boxing champion.

A full formal education is something Hooper never had, but he has striven to see that others have. Although his education extended through only the seventh grade, he later received a teacher's certificate and conducted classes for a brief time at Woodlawn School in Georgia. And to-day, just outside Montgomery, Alabama, stands a private school that he was instrumental in founding, Hooper Academy.

Hooper Academy, which opened in 1970, is this man's pride and joy. It's a school boasting academic and athletic excellence. A total of 310 students, boys and girls, were en-rolled in the school, from kindergarten through the twelfth grade, during the 1993–94 term. Keenly interested in the school's activities, Hooper likes to meet the students and usually attends the football homecoming game and graduation ceremonies.

The school's nickname? Naturally enough, the Colts.

The Miami Heart Institute has been another big part of Hooper's life. He has devoted considerable time and energy to the hospital and research facility, and served as its chairman of the board from 1975 to early 1993.

"At Hooper Academy, we're trying to build hearts," Hooper has said, "and at Miami Heart we're trying to keep them working."

Hooper, whose father lived to be ninety-four, has lived a very active life and used to play golf with great enthusiasm, but a couple of back injuries in recent years have put an end to eighteen holes on the course, although he remains a superb putter.

"I love golf," he said. "I used to be a real good golfer."

Hooper was good enough that he drove Bobby Dodd, the former Georgia Tech football coach, away from the game. At least that's what Dodd told everybody.

It seems that after losing to Hooper in several straight golf games, Dodd decided his clubs needed a rest.

"Bob told the story that he put the clubs in his car and they rusted out in back of his car and that Fred Hooper stopped him from playing golf," said Hooper, grinning. "Bob was a pretty good golfer at one time. He was a wonderful person, and he was a great coach."

Hooper also played golf with baseball star Dizzy Dean and was a friend of longtime Alabama football coach Paul ("Bear") Bryant.

Alabama is where Hooper had his farm when he first started breeding Thoroughbreds.

The idea of bringing up racehorses in Alabama didn't exactly win applause from the Kentucky breeders. As a matter of fact, they told Hooper, "You must be crazy if you think you can raise a racehorse in Alabama."

Doing it his way, Hooper proved the Kentucky breeders wrong. He had a good measure of success in more than twenty years of raising horses at his Montgomery farm.

Hooper later decided to buy a farm in another state, but it wasn't Kentucky. "Too cold up there," he said. "I like warm weather. I just like it down here."

Hooper moved to his Ocala farm in 1966 and subsequently sold his spread in Alabama. "I like it here better because our weather is so much better than the Montgomery, Alabama, area," he said.

Hooper is proud of the racing record that the state of Florida has carved out. "We've done exceptionally well in winning stakes races with our Florida-breds," he said.

Although Hoop Jr. was the first Thoroughbred that he bought, Hooper had been around horses from his early years. "I was raised on a farm, and my father had horses that we plowed with and mules. We didn't know what a tractor was back in my kid days."

As a teenager in Georgia, Hooper liked to ride bucking horses. "I used to think I could ride anything."

Hooper once owned a half-Thoroughbred named Prince. "Ol' Prince was a tremendous speed horse," Hooper said. "He ran 55 times over a period of three years and won 49 races."

Those were match races that the horse won. For some of those races he was known as Prince, for others Royal Prince. "I used to run him in the name of Prince, and after he got to beating everybody, I put the Royal on him," said Hooper. "I just thought that he was entitled to a little something besides just Prince."

Hooper has cases loaded with trophies that are testimony to his plentiful successes in racing. He has so many trophies that he doesn't have room to display them all. Most of the trophies are in the condominium that he and his charming wife, Wanda, have in Bal Harbour, Florida.

Other trophies are in a room in his Ocala home, and a few are in the farm's office.

It was at a Keeneland sale in August of 1943 that Hooper made a decision that eventually led to the Derby trophy that Hoop Jr. won for him. In looking around at that sale, he spotted Hip No. 134, a yearling sired by Sir Gallahad III. The colt was a bay with a few white hairs in his forehead. "He just caught my eye, the way he walked and all," Hooper recalled. "Didn't have a lot of flesh on him. He just looked real smart. So I said to myself, 'I'm gonna own you.' And I bought him for $10,200."

The auctioneer, speaking to the clerk whose job it was to obtain the names of buyers, said, "That young-looking, dark-haired man in the second or third row got that one."

Hooper made other purchases at the sale, and, before the auction was over, many people at Keeneland knew his name. Before long, many people in the racing world would, too. Thanks to Hoop Jr., the $10,200 yearling purchase.

In the fall of his two-year-old season, after five races earlier in his campaign, Hoop Jr. was training at Hooper's farm in Montgomery. "Then I brought him to Hialeah and trained him all during the Hialeah meeting," said Hooper. "Never ran him. But I told various people, 'I'm gonna win the Derby.'"

Hoop Jr., who was named for Hooper's son, was sent to New York, and, in his first start of 1945, he went off as the 7–10 favorite at Jamaica. Hooper bet $10,000 to win on the colt, who finished fourth. Gallorette, a talented filly ridden by Arcaro, won the race, a six-furlong allowance.

In his next start, the Wood Memorial, Hoop Jr. was ridden by Arcaro. Hooper again bet $10,000 to win. "We had asked Eddie Arcaro to not go to the front," Hooper said. "Eddie went to the front immediately and stayed in front all the way. He said he couldn't hold the horse." Hoop Jr., who triumphed by 2½ lengths, paid $15.10 on a $2-win bet, providing Hooper with a profit of $65,500.

Then it was on to Kentucky for the Derby. "I'd rather win the Kentucky Derby than make a million dollars in my construction business," Hooper said before the race.

Hooper gave Arcaro these instructions for the Derby: "The track is muddy, and you and our racing colors and the horse will look a lot better without any mud. Just go to the front."

Breaking from the No. 12 post position in a field of sixteen, Hoop Jr. took an early lead and hit the finish line six lengths on top. Hooper had bet another $10,000 on his colt, who paid $9.40 for $2. Hooper thus went away $37,000 richer for his wager, not to mention the $64,850 in purse money.

In the Preakness, Hoop Jr. was sent off at 1.35–1, a price that was too short to ignite Hooper's gambling instincts. Hoop Jr. finished second and suffered an injury in the race that ended his career after only nine races, the fewest number of starts ever for a Derby winner. "He got crowded kinda into the rail, and he overreached and hit himself and bowed," Hooper said.

"In my opinion, if Hoop Jr. had not gotten hurt in the Preakness, he would have been one of the top horses in racing history. He could run fast and go a distance with no problem. Eddie said that after the finish of the Derby he was just getting ready to run. I personally didn't think any horse could beat him. He could do anything a racehorse should do."

Hooper's next Derby starter was Olympia, a colt whose intense speed led to a match race early in his three-year-old season. Hooper was approached with the idea of matching Olympia against Stella Moore, a fleet quarter horse mare.

Hooper knew a thing or two about match races, having won all those events with Prince (a.k.a. Royal Prince), and he agreed to the Olympia-Stella Moore duel at Tropical Park. He suggested that each side ante up $50,000, but the quarter horse camp wanted to put up $25,000.

If the purse money wasn't all he wanted it to be, Hooper still had the prospect of wagering his money against any and all takers, the same way it had been done in the old days when two men with two fast horses would bet each other in a match race.

Hooper was told by the quarter horse people that they would bet all the money that he wanted to cover. "They were right in the amount that these quarter horse people wanted to bet," said Hooper. "I took everybody's bet and ended up with $93,000 on Olympia against the quarter horse."

Some Thoroughbred trainers, including Calumet Farm's Ben A. Jones, told Ivan Parke, the conditioner of Olympia, that he was foolish to think he could beat Stella Moore. "One day just two or three days before the match race was run," said Hooper, "a groom from Calumet Farm's barn came up there with a thousand dollars and said to Ivan Parke, 'We want to bet on the quarter horse.' I said, 'Ivan, let me have that money. That's Ben Jones' money.' I told this groom, 'Go back and tell Ben send some more money up. I have some more left.'"

Olympia won the race, a quarter-mile dash, and Hooper walked away with $93,000 in bets, as well as $25,000 in stakes.

"The quarter horse people were a great bunch," said Hooper. "They were the finest people as far as sports. They never grumbled."

Hooper told them if they wanted to wait a couple of days he'd run another one of his horses and give them a chance to get their money back. "They told me that they had had enough," said Hooper. "They didn't want to bet against me again."

The Fred Hooper of 1949, of course, was a middle-aged

man willing to gamble and run a horse of his in a match race. But would the mature, the venerable Fred Hooper of 1984, who knew from many experiences that anything can happen in a horse race, would *this* Fred Hooper run a horse of his in a match now?

Know something? Johnny Nerud was right about Fred Hooper. Showing that he still had that competitive spirit of his younger days, Hooper didn't blink an eye and replied, "Yeah, I've got a horse right now I'd run with anybody. That horse Precisionist, he is a fast horse."

That horse Olympia, he was a fast horse, too, and when the 1949 Derby rolled around, he was so highly regarded that he was sent off as the odds-on favorite. He led for more than a mile but tired and finished sixth.

Hooper is 6 feet, 4 inches tall, but in Ben A. Jones' eyes the man stood taller than ever the evening of the 1949 Derby. Hooper had planned a party after the race, and he went ahead and held it, even if it wasn't a victory celebration. Jones, who won the Derby with Ponder, was an invited guest at the party and was impressed by the way Hooper handled the affair.

"He's a big man, but he raised himself two inches in my estimation that night," Jones said. "It must have been a big disappointment to him—I should know, I've had many of them in my time—but you would never have known it by looking and talking to Hooper. He's a real sportsman."

Looking back on Olympia's performance in the 1949 Derby, Hooper said, "He was not really a mile-and-a-quarter horse."

Even so, he was a fine racehorse and, in retirement, an outstanding sire. "I've always liked speed," said Hooper. "You can get out of a lot of trouble if you've got speed. Olympia was a speed horse, and he was the foundation to my breeding."

Olympia proved to be an influential broodmare sire,

and two of his daughters were the mothers of Crozier and Admiral's Voyage, the last two Derby starters for Hooper.

In 1961, Crozier set a track record of 1:34³/₅ in capturing the one-mile Derby Trial at Churchill Downs. Hooper came close to winning the Derby that year, but Crozier was overtaken near the end and lost by three-quarters of a length to Carry Back. These two horses met ten times in a fierce rivalry, and Carry Back finished ahead of Crozier in seven of those races. Even so, Hooper believes to this day that if his jockey, Baeza, had waited longer before making his move in the Derby with Crozier, "why, Carry Back would *never* have beaten him."

Hooper's colors—blue, with a white *H* in a circle, white shoulder straps, red sleeves, and blue and red cap—are appropriate because his stable formerly raced all over the country. Recently, his stable has reduced its numbers and has concentrated on racing primarily in the East.

Hooper, who traditionally has more than a little input in the operation of his stable, has never regretted getting involved in the Thoroughbred business. "Not at all," he said. "I've had a lot of pleasure and enjoyment out of breeding them. These horses are just like second children to me. You have the dam, the granddams, and the grandpapas and all that on down."

Hooper has raced two champions—Susan's Girl and Precisionist.

Susan's Girl, enshrined in racing's Hall of Fame, was named champion three-year-old filly in 1972 and champion handicap filly or mare in 1973 and 1975. She earned $1,251,667 in her brilliant career.

"She was a great racemare, a great racemare," said Hooper.

Susan's Girl captured the Kentucky Oaks in 1972, a race that Hooper also won with My Portrait in 1961 and Quaze Quilt in 1974.

Precisionist received the Eclipse Award as champion sprinter of 1985.

Hooper also bred Tri Jet, who set a Saratoga track record of 1:47 for a mile and an eighth in winning the 1974 Whitney Stakes (bettering the old mark by a full 1^1/$_5$ seconds). Tri Jet, out of the Olympia mare Haze, later became a successful sire. His offspring have included Copelan, winner of six stakes races and earner of $594,278, and Tri to Watch. The latter, a 7^1/$_2$-length winner of the 1991 Champagne Stakes at Belmont Park, came to Churchill Downs for the Breeders' Cup Juvenile that fall but finished eighth at 5–1 odds.

Fred Hooper is no longer the "young-looking, dark-haired man" who showed up unannounced at the 1943 Keeneland sale. His hair is mostly white now, and he's not in perfect health. But he's not one to sit idly by and, before long during the 1984 interview, he got up from his chair and asked a visitor from Kentucky if he'd like to take a tour of the farm.

On a drive around the farm, Hooper pointed out his training track.

Hooper designed and built all the barns on the farm. He didn't study any other farm operation. He just did it his way. "I never paid any attention to what the other fellow had," he said. "I have my own ideas of what I want to do, and so long as I have no partner, why, I can go ahead and do it."

In an open area approximately midway between the two training barns is a beautiful marble stone over the grave of Hoop Jr. The horse died in 1964 and was buried in Alabama. When Hooper moved to Ocala, Hoop Jr.'s bones were dug up and reburied on the farm in Florida. On Hooper's seventy-fifth birthday, his four children—a son and three daughters—gave him the marble stone as a surprise present.

In mapping out his breeding philosophy, Hooper didn't

study anybody else's program. "Just went on my own idea, and it worked," he said.

The idea of going to a sale and spending millions of dollars for a single yearling is unthinkable for Hooper. "I wouldn't dare do it because there's so many of these horses that never win a race," he said. "I think it's ridiculous those prices they pay for them.

"Of course, that's none of my business. It's their money and not mine. Doesn't affect me."

Hooper chuckled.

"I get so much more pleasure out of my own breeding than I do in buying," Hooper said. "It's a different feeling to win with your own breeding than it is to buy one and win with it. Just like when my son was playing football. Other boys could make great plays. He played in the line, and he'd break through there and catch the quarterback, throw him for a loss, and it'd give you *that* feeling, you know, where if somebody else did it, it didn't amount to that much."

Crozier sired Precisionist, Journey at Sea, Advance Man, and other good horses for Hooper, most of them known for their soundness. "I had a lot of Croziers that ran good," Hooper said. "And his broodmares are turning out to be producing for me. He was really a good stud, I think."

It's said that two-year-old racehorses can keep a man young, especially the prospect of one of them developing into a Derby contender. In 1993, Mrs. Hooper was asked if her husband still dreams of winning the Derby again.

"Oh, yes," she replied. "That's his desire. Matter of fact, he just loves winning a race. He loves to be a winner. It gives him a great deal of satisfaction."

If Fred W. Hooper ever does win a second Kentucky Derby, it will have taken him a lot longer to reach that Churchill Downs infield winner's circle than the first time.

But he's never quit trying for another Derby victory. That's the charm of the Derby—and that's the competitiveness of Fred W. Hooper.

Flip Sal, a 9–1 shot ridden by Angel Cordero, Jr., won the first division of the Wood Memorial in 1974. (Photo by Bob Coglianese, courtesy New York Racing Association)

Trainer Steve DiMauro with Flip Sal. (Photo by Joseph DeMaria, courtesy New York Racing Association)

5

Flip Sal: A Derby "Winner" Every Step of the Way

LED FROM HIS STALL, the horse tossed his head in the air, as if to say, "Hey, y'all, follow me." Walking majestically, he was taken to his paddock at Red Oak Farm.

The groom opened the gate to the paddock, and the horse, glistening in the bright Florida sun, galloped off for the far corner where he could look over the fence at mares grazing in a nearby field. An equine version of girl-watching.

A visitor from Kentucky walked around the paddock to the far corner, trying to get the horse's attention. The horse swished his tail and approached the visitor, sticking his head over the fence and allowing his forehead to be petted. He was friendly enough, but his main attention was still directed to those mares in the field.

"He's quite a ladies' man," said proud owner Sal Tufano.

Flip Sal never had it so good.

You remember Flip Sal, the 1974 Kentucky Derby winner.

Oh, a purist might argue that Flip Sal didn't triumph in the Derby, but a sentimentalist will always believe that this horse came out of the 1974 Run for the Roses the biggest winner in the race. Flip Sal broke down badly in the Derby and was unable to finish, but he wound up winning the most important race he ever ran in—the race for his life.

One of twenty-three starters in the wild 100th Derby, Flip Sal was sent off as a 58–1 long shot. He came onto the track to the strains of "My Old Kentucky Home" and left in a horse ambulance. He was no favorite in the race, nor was he a good bet at first to survive his ordeal. But because of his intelligence and courage, Flip Sal recovered, and in 1979 when he was visited by this writer, the eight-year-old stallion was serving stud duty in sunny Florida.

Flip Sal, a steel-gray colt in 1974, was almost white in 1979. He had a left front ankle that was much larger than normal, but otherwise the horse was doing quite well.

That this was the same horse who came so close to dying was enough to bring cheer to the heart of any animal lover. That he was alive and well just proved that horses, like people, can overcome adversity. That he was enjoying the life of a stallion was something to behold when you consider that several other well-known horses from his crop—horses whose futures were much more promising than Flip Sal's during his darkest hour—had since died at early ages: Bushongo, impressive winner of the 1974 Flamingo, was destroyed in 1975; Protagonist, the champion two-year-old colt of 1973, died in 1976; Hudson County, the Kentucky Derby runner-up, was destroyed in 1976; and Destroyer, the Santa Anita Derby winner who finished sixth in the Kentucky Derby, was put to sleep in 1979.

Meanwhile, Flip Sal was frolicking in his paddock, generally living the life of Riley. He was getting around just fine—and without the aid of crutches. "He's still got that speed, with that leg and all," Tufano proudly said. "When the weather gets a little cool or whatever, the first step or so it seems like he'll favor it, and then, boom, he'll kinda walk out of it. I guess like an arthritic condition that you or I might have. But he doesn't show any limp at all."

Flip Sal's offspring were chips off the old block. Many of them were all gray, and they inherited a good measure of ability from their sire. In addition, many of them had "Flip" as part of their names.

In 1980 interviews, jockeys were impressed with Flip Sal's progeny.

"They're all really good-mannered horses, every one of them," said Gregg McCarron, a Maryland jockey. "They're just as sweet as can be to be around, they all gallop just as kind as can be, and yet when you put them to the test, they're there."

Eddie Maple, who rode Flip Sal in the 1974 Derby, also liked what he saw of the offspring. "They all seem to look somewhat like him, especially in color, and they run pretty darn good," said Maple.

Flip Sal's mishap in the Derby was an emotional experience for Maple, who had a special place in his heart for the horse. Maple, who sent Flip Sal a box of carrots after the '74 Derby, tried to keep up with the way the horse's sons and daughters were running. "I do watch 'em," Maple said. "I guess there's some kind of sentimental thing there."

Richard Small, a Maryland trainer, had a number of Flip Sal offspring in his care. He, too, spoke favorably of them—their willingness, their speed, and their readiness to run right off the bat.

"They're all real fast," he said. "And talk about 'try'— they all *really* try hard. They're just dead honest, and they always run good the first one or two times they run."

From Flip Sal's first crop, which began racing in 1978, came Flip for Betsy, who ran second in the 1979 Bryn Mawr Stakes at Keystone. Flip for Betsy was bred by Allan and Kevin Lavin, sons of highly respected Kentucky veterinarian Gary Lavin, the man mainly responsible for helping to pull Flip Sal through his crisis. Flip for Betsy was named for the Lavin boys' mother.

Gary Lavin saw Flip Sal in Ocala in 1978. The horse looked "terrific, just terrific," Lavin said. "He was so obstreperous that it concerned me that he might get to doing more than he should. But he was a little smarter than the average bear to begin with, so I'm sure he's learned how to use it. It's a nasty-looking ankle, but it's got to be as solid as the Rock of Gibraltar and he's learned how to use it.

"The way he looks now is kinda like what they asked Maurice Chevalier when he hit—what?—80 years of age, and they asked him how he felt. And he said, well, it was much better than the *alternative*. That holds true for Flip Sal and Hoist the Flag and a couple of those others that have kinda beat the odds."

Indeed, the odds were not in Flip Sal's favor after he broke down. The day after the Derby, Lavin thought Flip Sal had only about a twenty percent chance of making it— "and that was stretching it pretty good," he said.

Flip Sal suffered multiple fractures of the sesamoid bones in his left front ankle. There was nothing neat about the injury. "It was like smashing a Coke bottle on the road," said Lavin.

Despite everything he had going against him, Flip Sal did make it, thanks to expert veterinary care and his ideal temperament.

The horse was a perfect patient, "a veterinarian's delight," said Lavin. "He was a most cooperative horse. And he was very, very intelligent, much more intelligent than your average horse."

But Flip Sal did encounter problems on his road to recovery.

"We had him in a great big plaster cast from the bottom of his knee down, including the foot," Lavin said, "and he rubbed some big pressure sores on the back of the ankle, which we expected. All of them do it. Flip Sal went through all that, but every time we really thought we were getting backed up in the corner, he kinda made an end run and came through it. We worried about it more than anything else because there's not a whole lot to do other than to keep him comfortable.

"Of course, there are medications and treatments to keep some of the swelling down and some of the pain, but at the same time you don't want to take all the pain away because you want the horse to realize that he's in a dire situation. And Flip Sal couldn't have been better through the whole affair. All through that summer, as hot as it got, I guess through the whole affair, he might have lost 50 pounds, which is just remarkable."

The outpouring of affection, interest, and love for that horse was overwhelming. People from all parts of the world sent prayers and get-well cards and money to Flip Sal, who spent four months recovering at the Twin Spires Equine Clinic on the Churchill Downs property. Lavin estimated that at least three hundred or four hundred cards and letters were sent to the horse. "And from kids—that was the remarkable thing about it," Lavin said. "Every day for weeks, there'd be a stack of them at the stable gate. We got carrots, pennies, and quarters. We got cards from Iceland. We got 'em from Korea. It was remarkable."

An example of his mail was this letter from a thirteen-year-old admirer from Hollis, New York:

> Dear Flip Sal,
>
> I hope you feel better. I was almost crying when I saw you break down in the Derby and I sure hope you live a long time (by the way I bet you in the Derby and used to bet you in Aqueduct all the time).
>
> Sure hope you feel better.
>
> Dear Doctor,
>
> Please don't destroy him cause he is such a nice and beautiful race horse. Can you send me a picture of him so I can remember him?
>
> Thank you,
> Doreen Schmidt
>
> P.S. I'm a little girl and I love horses. I'm gonna become a jockey. I would like to have Flip Sal.

Flip Sal's fans continued to send him Christmas cards, birthday cards, and letters, almost as if they expected him to be able to read their messages.

But, then, maybe he could. After all, his "signature" did appear in a brochure announcing the beginning of his stud career. The announcement read, in part:

> My name is Flip Sal, and I'd like to take a moment of your time to tell you what I have planned for my future.
>
> You might recall I had a bit of a problem with a leg, but I'm happy to report that thanks to Dr. Gary Lavin and Dr. Bob Copelan that is all just history now. It seems I took a bad step in the running of the Kentucky Derby. I'm really sorry about that. I guess I did have some people worried for a time and lots of them sent me many nice letters.
>
> Some folks who don't know me even thought I'd never make it. How silly. Didn't they realize I have the blood of champions pumping through my veins and I had been in much tougher races, when I had met and defeated the best of my generation . . .

In summary, Flip Sal predicted, "I think I am going to enjoy this stallion business." He signed off with: "Thanks, Flip Sal."

Flip Sal, bred in Kentucky by Lee Eaton's Eaton Farm, Inc., and Marvin Waldman's and Samuel Lyon's Red Bull Stable, was purchased for $21,500 by Ben Cohen at Saratoga's 1972 yearling sale. Flip Sal was owned throughout his racing career by Cohen and Tufano, a New York insurance executive who purchased a half-interest in the colt soon after the Saratoga auction.

Flip Sal came into the Derby off a victory in the first division of the Wood Memorial. His time was slow—1:51$\frac{2}{5}$ for the mile and one-eighth on a fast track—and his final eighth was a dawdling fourteen seconds. In the second division, Rube the Great triumphed in 1:49$\frac{3}{5}$, some nine lengths better than Flip Sal's time. Had Flip Sal run in Rube the Great's division, he would have been defeated decisively enough that his camp would have had a hard time justifying sending him to Louisville, and thus he wouldn't have broken down in the Derby.

As it was, Flip Sal won his division of the Wood and it was a wide-open Derby, so he came to Louisville. His first-place check of $69,360 in the Wood was more than he had earned previously in his busy, busy career. He had embarked on his career on February 20, 1973, at Hialeah Park and won for the first time, in an Aqueduct maiden claiming event, on May 10 of that year while running for a $27,500 tag. He triumphed once more as a juvenile, capturing a six-furlong allowance at Belmont Park. Going into the Derby, Flip Sal had run in all of twenty-four races, including eighteen in his two-year-old season. From 1971 through 1993, no other Derby starter has entered the race with that many lifetime outings.

Following the '74 Derby, Flip Sal won the hearts of many admirers with the recovery from his injury. In 1979, the last time this writer saw Flip Sal, things were looking rosier than ever for the horse. And, speaking of roses, Tufano would have liked nothing better than to see one of Flip Sal's offspring complete some unfinished business.

It seems that the highly regarded Drone, who sired Flip Sal, was unbeaten but was hurt a month or so before the 1969 Kentucky Derby and never raced again. Sir Gaylord, the sire of Drone, was favored for the 1962 Derby but suffered an injury the day before the race and was retired. Turn-to, the sire of Sir Gaylord, was the 1954 Derby's winter-book favorite but bowed a tendon, an injury that ended his career.

So after standout colts in three previous generations of his family had gone wrong on their way to the Derby, Flip Sal made it to the race—but he didn't finish it.

That's the unfinished work that Tufano wanted to complete.

"I feel it's only a matter of time before one of his offspring

Flip's Pleasure, a daughter of Flip Sal, won nine stakes in her career, including (from top right, clockwise) the Ticonderoga Handicap in 1984 and the Top Flight, Next Move, Ticonderoga, and Iroquois in 1985. (Courtesy New York Racing Association)

will make it into the Derby," Tufano said. "He's just shown that much, that one of them will make it. One of them in that line is going to run—and run big—in that race."

It would have had the makings of a Hollywood movie script for one of Flip Sal's offspring to run in the Derby— but, alas, that story line was never to play out on the hallowed grounds of Churchill Downs.

Flip Sal, who needed a travel agent to keep up with his many shifts in residence as a stallion, originally served stud duty in Kentucky, then went to Florida and later New York before returning to Kentucky in the fall of 1981. He ended his days in New York again, and on June 6, 1985, at the age of fourteen, he died of an apparent heart attack while breeding a mare. Standing his first season at Blue Sky Farm, near Middletown, New York, Flip Sal had been in excellent health up until the time of his death. He was buried next to his paddock.

All told, he would sire sixteen stakes winners from 185 foals. His stakes winners were B. C. Sal, Carla's Love, Eminently Proper, Flip for Luck, Flip for Ross, Flippable, Flip's Pleasure (who won nine stakes and earned $603,636), Flip's Serenade, Grey Bucket, He's a Flip, Hidden Capital, Important Memo, Silver Comet, Strike Us Rich, The Flips Comin, and What a Flip.

Perhaps Grey Bucket best epitomized Flip Sal's determination. Especially that determination to live.

Grey Bucket, born at the One Potato Two Potato Farm in Florida, survived a near-fatal injury, just as his sire did. He was a 1982 Kentucky Derby nominee but didn't start in the race. Still, the fact that he ever started at all was a story in itself.

As a yearling in 1980, Grey Bucket was romping through a paddock and ran into a bolt that was sticking out a few inches from a post that a gate was hanging on. "He went flying by it and hit it and tore his side wide open," said Bill Crocker, who bred the colt. "You could reach inside of him and grab his ribs."

It took veterinarian Ed Noble hours to clean and sew up the gaping wound. "He had rust all inside him—rust that came off the bolt," said Crocker.

The outlook for Grey Bucket was dark. "He stood in shock for four days," said Crocker. "We just had resigned ourselves that we were going to lose him."

But Grey Bucket, like his old man, made it through the ordeal. "After he came out of his shock, he came out of it beautifully," said Crocker. "The vet said another eighth of an inch [longer] and he wouldn't have survived the first day. It would have gone into his intestines."

Grey Bucket, who carried a huge scar from his days at the Florida farm, was sold for $40,000 at the 1981 Ocala Breeders' Sales Company's two-year-old-in-training auction. He probably would have brought a higher price if it hadn't been for the scar. One person who was involved in the bidding, but stopped because of the scar, was Steve DiMauro, who trained Flip Sal for both of his victories as a three-year-old (an allowance race and then a division of the Wood Memorial).

"The scar scared me," said DiMauro, who would win the Morven Stakes in 1981 with Grey Bucket and train the colt for part of his 1982 season.

The nasty scar, nearly two feet long on Grey Bucket's left side, was covered by his saddlecloth in races. "He wears it well," DiMauro said with a chuckle early in the colt's career.

Grey Bucket launched his career in the spring of 1981 at Keeneland and won by 7½ lengths as a 27–1 long shot. In his next start, the roan colt captured the Lafayette Stakes as the 3–5 favorite at Keeneland. Grey Bucket, who had been trained by Magnus Fairley, then was sent to DiMauro in New York.

Comparing Grey Bucket to Flip Sal, DiMauro said in

early 1982: "He's got an extremely good temperament. His father was the same. That's what saved him."

Grey Bucket was weighted at 110 pounds on the Experimental Free Handicap, but his two-year-old campaign (four victories, including two in stakes, and earnings of $71,176) turned out to be the best season of his career. He won only two of thirty-nine races in the next five years.

Although Flip Sal never had an offspring to run for the roses, he may turn up one of these years as the grandsire or great-grandsire of a horse not only to start in the Derby but to win it.

That would be a remarkable finish to the story of a remarkable horse—Flip Sal.

6

... And Here Comes Silky!

TELEVISION, IN THE 1950s. Squirming teenagers were watching Elvis Presley do likewise on "The Ed Sullivan Shewww." Preschool kiddies were all eyes and oversized ears for "The Mickey Mouse Club" and its No. 1 television Mouseketeer, Annette. Millions were watching Jackie Gleason winging across the screen, giving out with "And *awwaay* we go!" And, on Saturday afternoons, baseball fans were tuning in for the Game of the Week and listening to announcer Dizzy Dean butcher the King's English and sing out with the "Wabash Cannonball."

On May 3, 1958, television covered another popular show, one that had millions of viewers anxiously watching from across the country. It was the Silky Sullivan Show, although Churchill Downs ran it under another name— the Kentucky Derby.

The eighty-fourth Derby was proudly presented by the Gillette Cavalcade of Sports, which also brought you such other events as the Preakness and Belmont Stakes, the World Series, the All-Star baseball game, the Rose Bowl, the Blue-Gray football game, and the featured Fight of the Week every Friday night. All of this was Gillette's way of saying "thank you" for using its products, which included a choice of three razors—light, regular, and heavy.

Commercials aside, Silky Sullivan was the main attraction—the golden glamour boy—of the 1958 Derby, and television was making an all-out effort to cover his every

Silky Sullivan, shown at Santa Anita Park, was a "real pet around the barn, a horrible moocher of carrots," The Thoroughbred of California reported in 1958. "When he comes back from a race, a dozen or more men compete to see who'll get to wash him off and cool him out." (Santa Anita Park Photo)

move. Silky was so special that the Columbia Broadcasting System used a split-screen technique for the race. For certain parts of the race, most of the screen was for the leaders while the lower right corner was set aside for Silky alone, running far behind the pack. Viewers watched and waited for Silky, their hero, to make his expected come-from-behind charge.

Silky had staged many such charges during his colorful career. His style was unique, almost as if it were the product of a Hollywood scriptwriter's imagination. Silky would dawdle far, far behind the field before launching his patented stretch run that would sail him past the leaders.

His rallies were unbelievable. . . . He surged from twenty-seven lengths behind to win the one-mile Golden Gate Futurity by three-quarters of a length. . . . He trailed by $37\frac{1}{2}$ lengths in the $1\frac{1}{16}$-mile California Breeders' Champion Stakes and lost by just a neck, his final quarter of a mile being clocked in an incredible $21\frac{2}{5}$ seconds. Eddie Arcaro, who rode the front-running Old Pueblo to victory in this race, said that when he looked over his right shoulder early in the homestretch, Silky wasn't even in sight. One wit suggested that Arcaro merely had looked over the wrong shoulder. Silky, you see, was still over on the backstretch. . . .

He made up a deficit of forty-one lengths to score a breathtaking victory in a $6\frac{1}{2}$-furlong allowance race at Santa Anita Park. . . . And he captured the $1\frac{1}{8}$-mile Santa Anita Derby by $3\frac{1}{2}$ lengths after lagging $28\frac{1}{2}$ lengths behind the leader.

Clearly, a man with a heart condition had no business betting on Silky. Indeed, one of Silky's owners, Tom Ross, had a heart condition and wasn't permitted by his doctor to see all of the colt's races.

Silky was a box-office attraction who pulled in crowds in record numbers. For example, a throng of 61,123 turned out to watch him in the Santa Anita Derby, a record crowd for that race.

Symbolizing America's never-say-die spirit, Silky captured the imagination of the public in an unprecedented fashion. His name became a household word, and he received mail from all parts of the country, including letters from fans enclosing two dollars to pay for a few souvenir pieces of straw from Silky's bed. One racetrack—Golden Gate Fields—even provided a secretary to answer Silky's mail, causing a skeptic to wonder, "Can't he write his own letters?" A good question, since at least one newspaper story carried Silky's own byline.

Silky's size was imposing—he was tall and big with powerful muscles. A magnificent-looking chestnut colt, he was so striking in appearance that one writer suggested Silky would be an easy winner if there were body-beautiful contests for horses. Silky, to be sure, was a "picture horse," one who would appear on the track with his mane curled and his coat glistening.

He was hailed as the greatest Sullivan since John L., and he had such nicknames as The Red Comet, The Lovable Laggard, Mr. Heart Attack, and The California Comet.

Bill Shoemaker, who rode Silky in some of his memorable come-from-behind efforts, said nobody could rush the colt into gear in the early part of his races. "If you try to rush him, he'll sulk," Shoemaker said. "I think somebody named him Sulky Sullivan."

Actually, Silky's name stemmed from that of his sire, Sullivan, and his dam, Lady N Silk. Comedian George Kessel cracked that the colt's real name was Silky Solomon but that he had been horsenapped by the Irish.

His co-owners, Ross and Phil Klipstein, purchased Silky for $10,700 at a 1956 Del Mar yearling sale. During his heyday, they turned down offers reportedly ranging from $250,000 to $500,000. According to one story, a syndicate of Eastern businessmen offered Klipstein and Ross

$500,000 with the intention that Silky wouldn't race again for at least a year. The Easterners had the idea that they could make a bundle of money merely exhibiting Silky at fairs and capitalizing on his name to merchandise such items as Silky Sullivan T-shirts and various other gimmicks.

As fate would have it, a mouth cut saved Silky from the cruelest cut of all. Years later, trainer Reggie Cornell recalled that Klipstein, one of Silky's co-owners, had the idea that all colts should be gelded. Silky was one of ten or so of the stable's horses scheduled to be castrated, but beforehand he suffered a cut mouth. "Silky hooked his mouth, and it ripped the hell out of his mouth and we had to sew him up," said Cornell.

Cornell was advised by a veterinarian to wait a few days before gelding Silky.

"Okay," said Cornell, who didn't want to geld Silky anyway.

In the meantime, all the other horses were castrated. "Did you get these horses cut?" Klipstein asked Cornell.

"Yeah, they got cut," replied the trainer, never mentioning a word about Silky.

After Silky's mouth healed, he was taken to Santa Anita. "Old man Klipstein came and looked at him every day," said Cornell. "Never realized the son of a b---- wasn't cut. So we kept training him a little bit—eighths, quarters, and he could run right off the bat. But he always had a real bad-sounding way of breathing."

Cornell said that Kentucky veterinarian Alex Harthill claimed that "it could have been from when they pulled his tongue out to sew up his mouth, they held it so long it might have broken the fibers down in the top of his tongue."

Finally, Klipstein noticed one day that Silky was still all-man. Klipstein, whom Cornell described as "a funny old son of a b----" who'd "get mad at a lot of things," stooped down, inspecting Silky, and then said to the trainer, "Thought you cut this horse."

"Well, Mr. Klipstein," explained Cornell, "when we was gonna cut this horse, why, he cut his mouth, and I had to sew it up, so I just let him go."

"Well, g--------, I wanted him cut!" demanded Klipstein.

"Well, he isn't cut anyway," replied Cornell.

With that exchange, there was no more attempt to remove Silky's manhood, and the colt proceeded on with his training.

"G------, he could train," remembered Cornell. "Not *really* fast, but he could go out of that gate and he'd go five-eighths in 59 [seconds]."

Ron McAnally, a nephew of Cornell's, recalled in a 1993 interview that it was Silky Sullivan's early training that, in his opinion, led to his come-from-behind style of running. It seems that in 1957, while Cornell was in Northern California with his horses, McAnally, an assistant trainer with the stable, was at Hollywood Park with about twenty-five two-year-olds, including Silky Sullivan.

"I called Reggie one morning in San Francisco," McAnally said. "He wanted to know how the 2-year-olds were coming. I said, 'Reggie, you've got one colt here that's far better than any one of the others.' He asked me which one it was. I said, 'A colt by Sullivan.' He said, 'Well, why don't you just kinda break him behind horses and give the others a head start and then let him pick 'em up?' So I kept doing that and doing it, and I kept taking him back more and more because he kept getting better and better. He'd come along and catch them. We started out with a head start of two or three lengths, then we moved it back to five lengths and then moved it on back to 10. I really think to this day that that's how he learned his style of running. We did not train him intentionally to do that, but then he just probably thought that that's the way he was supposed to run."

George Taniguchi rode Silky in some of his early work-outs. "I had been working him and galloping him, and he was a very striking chestnut—good, stout, muscular," Taniguchi would say years later. "I *knew* that he could run. He had speed. But I didn't know exactly how good of a horse he was."

Silky's unveiling came on May 17, 1957, at Hollywood Park. Taniguchi, who had the mount on Silky, received the following instructions from Cornell: "George, this is a big fella. Now when the gate goes up, he'll break in front and maybe drop back a couple of lengths. Just let him poke along and when he gets ready to run, just let him run through the stretch."

Silky, a mild favorite, was among four first-time starters in a field of a dozen maiden two-year-olds going five furlongs. The other three horses making their debuts wound up running tenth, eleventh, and twelfth. And, for a while, it appeared that Silky was going to finish far back himself.

Contrary to Cornell's prediction, Silky didn't break in front. "He walked out of the gate," said Taniguchi. "He breaks and then he just stops and then he just lags back and lags back. I thought, well, he's not going to make it."

That slow start would always occupy a place in Cornell's memory bank. "He broke, took about three strides and he just started to come back, come back, come back," said the trainer.

Silky was eighth at a couple of early calls, which wasn't as far back as he would be in subsequent races, but it was still too much for Cornell to bear watching. To make matters worse, Cornell had brought Klipstein to the races that day.

Silky was "so far back that I just kinda turned," said Cornell. "I was gonna get away from old man Klipstein because I told him that son of a b---- was gonna run good. I turned and wasn't watching him when he left the quarter pole."

By that time, Silky was in gear. As Taniguchi said, "About the three-eighths pole, I just tapped him to see if he was going to show me that speed. He just literally flew and he showed the kind of a style, the kind of a race he wanted to run then. I didn't realize it; neither did Reggie."

What Cornell did realize that afternoon was that once he had turned his back on Silky, something was happening that had the crowd cheering wildly. Silky was rallying, but was still sixth at the stretch call, better than four lengths behind the leader. Silky was gaining with each stride, and now Cornell had turned back around and was taking it all in. "All at once I heard a roar and I looked up and they were just gettin' to about the sixteenth pole and you could see this son of a b---- was like a streak and he was getting by the last horse," said Cornell. "And I heard some guy say, 'G------, he got up in time.' I said, 'Shoot, there wasn't no way that that son of a b---- could get up in time.'

"Here he comes," Cornell went on, slapping his hands together, "G--------, he got him on the outside." Silky had won . . . by a nose.

Silky returned to the races twelve days later, again going off as the favorite in a five-furlong race at Hollywood. "I shouldn't have run him back," said Cornell. "He had a splint."

Taniguchi again was aboard Silky. "Reggie asked me to kinda hustle him out and lay a little closer," said Taniguchi.

Taniguchi recalled that Silky was "a lot closer" to the lead. "He broke good. I know I was a lot closer and he didn't finish well."

Actually Silky was thirteen to fourteen lengths back in sixth place for part of the race, which was a bigger deficit than he trailed by in his first start. But Taniguchi was right on one count: Silky didn't finish well. He came in fifth in a field of eight.

Silky was out of action for the next 5½ months. "I fired

the splint," said Cornell, "and took him down to Del Mar, and then we just took him out in the ocean every day and kept him going down there."

From the ocean in Southern California, Silky then was sent to the northern part of the state. One morning in the track kitchen at Tanforan, Cornell was introduced to Manuel Ycaza, a young jockey from Panama. "He couldn't speak good English," recalled Cornell, "and I said, 'Ycaza, I got three good colts there to work. You go over. You pick out whatever one you want. I'm gonna get a cup of coffee, and I'll be back. I'm gonna work the three of them.' Yakky walked along and he looked at 'em all and he says, 'I get on this one.' And it was Silky. Took him out and breezed him. And he said, 'Now, I come over, get on him *every* morning, gallop him, and I would like to ride him for you.' I said, 'Okay.' So we get him ready and go over to Golden Gate Fields. Non-winners of two comes up, and I put Ycaza on him, and I said, 'Ycaza, this horse, when he won his race, he came from a good ways back. Don't really get excited on him because I'm sure'—'Oh,' he says, 'you no have to tell me how to ride him. I'm on him all the time. I know what he can do.' I said, 'Okay.'"

Ycaza indeed had gotten to know all about Silky. The colt lagged back in last place, trailing by twelve lengths at one point, before he began running for Ycaza in the stretch. Silky won the six-furlong allowance by a length and three-quarters. His time was 1:09²/₅.

Silky demonstrated the same running style in his next race, but he didn't win this time. Far back in the Berkeley Handicap, he closed ground through the stretch and finished third.

A week later he came from last to win a six-furlong allowance again in 1:09²/₅ at Golden Gate. He trailed by seventeen lengths in that race. In his next race, he launched a rally that carried him to victory in the Golden Gate Futurity. Making his final start at two, Silky rushed from twenty-five lengths back to finish fourth, beaten by 4³/₄ lengths, in the California Breeders' Trial Stakes, a race won by Old Pueblo.

Silky launched his three-year-old season with a fifth-place finish in a six-furlong Santa Anita allowance, followed by a neck victory at a mile six days later at the Arcadia, California, track. Cornell recalled that Eddie Arcaro was watching the latter race from a box seat. "I said to Arcaro, 'You want to bet a hundred dollars on a horse that's got a helluva chance in here?' And he says, 'Who's that?' I said, 'Silky Sullivan.' So he turned around to his agent, and he said, 'Here, take a hundred to win and a hundred to show.'"

Cornell said that while Silky was slow-gaiting it in the early going Arcaro "just turned around to me and he said, 'That's a fine son of a b---- that *you* touted me on, isn't it?'"

The next thing Arcaro knew, Silky was surging to the lead in the final sixteenth in an eye-popping display of stretch power. He paid $6.90, $4.60, and $2.80 across the board, a $285 profit for Arcaro. The veteran jockey also profited from watching the race. Arcaro was riding against Silky in the colt's next start, the $67,360 California Breeders' Champion Stakes at Santa Anita. Arcaro had the mount on Old Pueblo, an odds-on favorite who took the lead early in the 1¹/₁₆-mile race. "When he come to the head of the stretch, he's about six in front," said Cornell. "Arcaro never looked for nothin'. He just put his head down and he said, 'I hit that son of a b---- every time he hit the ground because I knew that red b------ was gonna come and get him.'" Sure enough, Silky came powering along in the stretch, only to lose by a neck.

Joe Burnham was shooting a film of the California Breeders' Champion Stakes, and Frank Tours, who worked in the Santa Anita publicity department, was keeping him abreast of Silky Sullvan's whereabouts during the race. "When we got to about the half-mile, I was still on Old

Pueblo," Burnham recalled. "Arcaro was going along in front easy."

The alert Tours advised Burnham, "Don't worry. You don't have to pan back to Silky Sullivan. He's got no chance."

Burnham recalled: "So as I got to the quarter pole, I noticed that Arcaro was looking behind and sorta driving the horse. I'm following Arcaro, wondering why he's hitting this horse because it looks to me he's six in front and nobody else is in the picture. And Tours starts saying, 'Joe, you should see this. You should see this.' And then at the last instant, as Old Pueblo is winning the race, another horse comes in—and it's only about five frames in the picture. You could barely see him go through."

Bill Shoemaker next rode Silky for the first time, and the two hit it off quite well. Oh, forget the fact that Silky appeared hopelessly beaten in a 6½-furlong allowance at Santa Anita. Said Cornell: "I thought he pulled up." Said Klipstein: "I thought he was just left at the gate." Appearances can be deceiving, and Silky steamrollered from forty-one lengths back to win by a half-length. He covered the last quarter in 22²/₅ seconds on a track listed as good. Shoemaker then guided Silky to his memorable triumph in the Santa Anita Derby, turning a 28½-length deficit into a 3½-length victory.

The Thoroughbred of California, in its account of the Santa Anita Derby, told its readers: "We do solemnly promise to restrain ourselves in this review. We vow faithfully to write of Silky Sullivan as if he were a horse. Which is ridiculous."

Silky later was sent to Golden Gate Fields. "These people made a commitment that they would take him to San Francisco," Cornell said of Silky's owners, "and I didn't want to take him to San Francisco. I wanted to take him to Phoenix or someplace halfway and train him right after the Santa Anita Derby and then go into Keeneland. But they made a commitment that they were going to take him to San Francisco. Got up there and, son of a b----, it rained for 30 days and 30 nights. Well, there was nothin' you could do. You had to go through the mud. Instead of workin' your horse the way you wanted, you had to go around mud holes and the horse just got fat and he got behind."

He ran on Friday, April 11 at Golden Gate Fields, and on the day of that race the *San Francisco Examiner* proclaimed in a headline: "Watch Your Heart—Silky Zooms Today!" The largest weekday crowd—19,102—in the track's history turned out, but the overweight Silky didn't zoom enough. He finished third as the 3–10 favorite in a mile allowance. "Silky needed that race bad," Cornell said afterward. "That race will help him a lot, and with a seven-eighths-of-a-mile race coming up at Churchill Downs, he'll be real fit for the big one."

Silky then was shipped to Kentucky.

No horse ever reached Louisville with more pre-Derby ballyhoo than Silky. After a seven-hour, forty-three–minute flight from San Francisco, where he was given a big sendoff by school children and other fans, Silky hit Louisville like a Hollywood star, with an entourage of two stablemates, a pony, a groom, a stable boy, a veterinarian, an exercise boy, and his trainer. Also on the plane was another Derby horse named Gone Fishin'.

"Silky came with fire-engine red stable traps, leg bandages, bridle, and noseband, 1,200 pounds of bunched muscle that required special security measures to keep some 4,000 fans who visited his stall at Churchill Downs from pulling hairs from his tail," *The Blood-Horse* magazine would recall years later.

George Koper, a former Louisville newspaperman who now is the claims clerk at Churchill Downs, recalled the first morning that Silky Sullivan appeared on the track. "I was with Ben Masden, who was the *Daily Racing Form* clocker," Koper said, "and Silky Sullivan came back panting and gasping after he galloped. Ben said, 'If you see anybody that wants to bet on this horse, take it and give it to me.'"

Cliff Martin, a longtime Churchill Downs employee who saw his first Derby in 1913, would always remember Silky. "The best-looking horse ever I seen was Silky Sullivan," declared Martin, who tended the Downs' press box lunch counter for years. "Pretty as a picture."

But in appraising Silky's ability, Martin couldn't resist adding with a laugh, "He wasn't worth two dead flies."

Other Kentuckians were awed by Silky's appearance. The question of Silky's ability was secondary to his status as a celebrity.

In Louisville, soda fountains served up "Silky Sullivan Sundaes" and the West Coast wonder was the talk of the town.

Silky raced once in Kentucky before the Derby, starting a week beforehand in the seven-furlong Stepping Stone Purse. On his way from the stable to the paddock for the Stepping Stone, Silky was the center of attention as fans leaned against the fence to get a closeup look.

"Hey, *Silky!*"

"There he is!"

"Show 'em, Silky!"

"Here he comes!

"Did you ever see such a pretty tail?"

"Look at him. He's confident. He knows he's going to win."

"That's my horse! Hey, *Silky!*"

Silky was a tepid favorite in the field of six. "He brought a lot of people out that day," said Cornell. "Funny thing is, I was gonna run him in four flat shoes, but it looked like it was gonna rain and I had the shoes all made for him with little stickers on them."

Cornell said he gave the blacksmith specific instructions. "I said, 'Now whatever you do, don't leave this barn before the horse leaves the barn because if it happens to rain, I

want you to switch these shoes.' I come up about 3:30 and,
g------, it started rainin.'"

The blacksmith, however, had left the barn, although
Cornell had told him to remain. The track was rated as
good, and Silky, his mane and tail braided with bows of red
and green yarn, was all dressed up, even if he had on the
wrong kind of shoes.

"Well, I knew he could run a little in slop, but he couldn't
run over a heavy track," said Cornell. "That son of a b----,
I'll tell you something, when he broke and came out of the
seven-eighths chute, he was with his horses—just even
with his horses—and when he made that little drop down
on the main track, he got to just kinda floundering and
when he got to the five-eighths pole, instead of the people
hollerin' for him, they started laughin'. Now when he got
to the half-a-mile pole, it was like goin' to a circus. Them
son of a b------ was laughin'.

"So J---- C-----, I thought, Shoemaker, what the hell, you
ever gonna move on this sucker? So he gets over to the
three-eighths pole, no move. Farther back and farther out
in the middle of the racetrack. Well, when he turned for
home, I could just see him when he straightened around,
Shoemaker hit him once and here he come. Well, a horse
called Benedicto was bearin' out, and he made old Silky
alter his course and the sucker just missed."

Despite the loss, Silky gained support from even some of
his staunchest critics. He roared from thirty-two lengths
behind to finish a flying fourth, beaten by just 2½ lengths.
He came through with such a fast finishing kick that one
clocking for his last eighth of a mile was a blazing $10^{2/5}$
seconds.

"Silky went out a mile and an eighth in 48," recalled
Cornell, exaggerating. Silky actually was eased up a mile
and an eighth in $1:51^{1/5}$ or $1:51^{2/5}$.

Anyway, Cornell added years later in looking back on
the Stepping Stone, "Shoe, just as soon as he got off him,

he said, 'They'll never beat this horse in the Derby.' But it never stopped rainin' from then on. It got muddy and muddy and muddy. And he couldn't run in the mud."

However, immediately after the Stepping Stone, Cornell couldn't look into the future and foresee that raindrops would keep falling in Louisville in the days leading up to the Derby. During Derby Week, there was at least a trace of rain each day and total precipitation measured 2.03 inches, including 0.11 of an inch on Derby Day.

Following the Stepping Stone, Cornell was jubilant. Back at the barn, he gave Silky a fistful of sugar. "Well, we showed those hardboots today we can run," Cornell said with a laugh.

Could this horse really win the Derby? Was he a legitimate contender? Or was he merely a pretender? Opinions differed.

One trainer, V. R. ("Tennessee") Wright, called Silky a "bleepin' cinch" to win the Derby.

One California professor, who used certain lecture periods to answer questions submitted by her students, was asked, "Will Silky Sullivan win the Kentucky Derby?" "The only way he can lose," she answered without even a trace of alarm, "is if 'The Shoe' falls off his back. Next question . . ."

Jimmy Breslin wrote that you addressed Silky as Himself. "Looking at this 1,200-pound beaut you forget all the raps hardboots put on him," Breslin wrote. "You wind up rooting for him to win the Kentucky Derby, just like everybody else. Horsemen keep insisting 'he won't be anywhere Derby Day,' but Himself was a grand sight while it lasted. If, indeed, it is about to be rubbed out."

Many people simply questioned whether Silky could fall far behind the caliber of horses he would face in the Derby and then try to make up that much ground on them.

But all this pre-race conjecture mattered not. Win or lose, the 1958 renewal was tagged "Silky's Derby"—and that's the way it would always be remembered.

Writers and photographers were drawn like magnets to Silky's barn at Churchill Downs. Newsmen rated him the all-time wordage winner in the history of the Derby. So great was Silky's popularity that Western Union reported that its press file was forty percent higher than for any previous running of the Derby.

Silky was a cover boy, his picture appearing on the front of *Sports Illustrated* in its Derby preview issue. *Life* magazine gave its seven million subscribers a half-dozen pages of Silky photos. "After dropping so far out of it his backers give up," *Life* told its readers, "he then subjects them to a different emotional strain, running like a horse with his tail on fire—and winning."

Silky loved the attention. On his way to the track he sometimes would stop at the sight of a camera aimed at him. He would even turn to give photographers his profile.

"He'll pose faster than Jayne Mansfield," wrote Arthur Daley of *The New York Times*.

Unlike most racehorses, Silky wasn't accustomed to rising early for his morning work. "He is like a banker," said Cornell. "He dislikes getting up early, so we work him just before they close the track."

As the Derby neared, rumors were circulating that Silky was ailing and was running a temperature. Awakened at his hotel in the early hours of Derby morning, the usually good-natured Cornell curtly told a caller, "Do you think I'd be sleeping if there was anything wrong with my horse?" With that, Cornell hung up the telephone with a bang.

Cornell had no way of knowing it at the time, but he would have been better off staying in bed rather than going to the track for the Derby.

They came from all over to watch Silky run for the roses. Women in sack dresses, men in flattops, the young and the old, the rich and the poor. Silky's many admirers in the crowd of 70,451 wagered $369,726 on him in the Derby, including a record number of $2 tickets. Much of the big money was going on Tim Tam, and the Maine Chance Farm entries of Jewel's Reward and Ebony Pearl. At post time the odds were 2–1 on the entry, and 2.10–1 on both Tim Tam and Silky.

When starter James Thomson pushed the button to send the field of fourteen on its way, Silky naturally was in no hurry. He dropped back, farther and farther, until at one point he was sauntering some thirty-two lengths behind the leader, Lincoln Road.

The crowd waited for Silky to make his move and, as the field hit the far turn, there was as much attention focused on you-know-who back in last place as there was on Lincoln Road and the other front-runners. Then it happened. Shoemaker asked Silky to turn it on. Silky immediately overtook a horse, Warren G., and the cry rang out from some of his backers, "Here comes Silky!"

But it was nothing more than an illusion. Silky went past Warren G. so quickly that Warren G. appeared to be going in slow motion. Little did onlookers realize at the time but Warren G. *was* moving in slow motion. The horse was tired—and hopelessly beaten—and his jockey, Ken Church, was beginning to ease him up when Silky went past. Silky was finally moving—but not nearly as powerfully as it first appeared.

As Church would say afterward, "Silky looked to me like he was laboring when he passed me."

Meanwhile, the real action was going on up front. Tim Tam, a Calumet Farm colt, was making his move while Ebony Pearl tried to take a bite out of another horse. Silky never got close enough to the leaders for a bite.

The long Churchill Downs stretch, where the script called for Silky to make history, instead was the end of the road for his press agents. The Red Comet fizzled and finished twelfth, a total of twenty lengths behind the victorious Tim Tam.

Tim Tam's time on a muddy track was 2:05; Silky's time

was 2:09²/₅, a far cry from the clocking he had predicted in a story he "told" to Orlo Robertson of *The Associated Press.* "As I've got it figured," said the story bylined by Silky, "I'll run the first half mile in around 50 seconds, the second half in about 49 and reel off the last quarter in 23. As I figure that'll make the time for the mile and one quarter in 2:02. I know that I'll probably be 30 or so lengths back midway of the back stretch, but keep your eyes on the flaming chestnut. That's me.

"Pete, he's Pete Kozar me exercise boy, tells me 2:02 isn't fast enough to win. No problem if it isn't. I'll just run that last quarter still faster."

Alas, Silky needed all of twenty-nine seconds to cover the last quarter. Pete, the exercise boy, could have run it faster.

Never has any horse received so much fanfare and run so poorly. For a horse who beat only two opponents, Silky came in for far, far more than his share of attention. Consider: Fred Capossela, who called the Derby for a nationwide television audience, mentioned Silky's name five times and Tim Tam's only once for the first mile and one-eighth of the race. By the time Capossela had called their names out for the last time as they crossed the finish line, the count was six for Silky, four for Tim Tam.

Although television viewers heard Silky's name half a dozen times from start to finish, they didn't see as much of him as they had anticipated. A spokesman for CBS said that Silky wasn't flashed on the split-screen setup as much as his fans would have liked "because he didn't run a good race. We gave him all the camera he deserved. After all, we were covering the Derby."

Bill Ladd, television editor for *The Courier-Journal* in Louisville, thought that the split-screen technique wasn't effective.

"The idea was pretty much wasted," Ladd wrote. "In the

first place, Silky never got into contention, so his position at any time was only a matter of academic interest.

"In the second place, Silky's private camera did not show his relation to the rest of the field. It just showed a horse out for a Saturday spin by himself, for all intents and purposes."

Cornell, the rotund trainer of Silky, didn't see much of his colt's Saturday spin. With so many people congested in the clubhouse, Cornell couldn't get from the paddock to his box seat—"I had to pay $380 for the box and never sat in the son of a b----," he complained—and wound up locating a vantage point where he managed to see only part of the race. Cornell said the condition of the track hurt Silky. "He didn't have no chance over that heavy racetrack," Cornell said. "He'da ran good if the track had been fast. I wouldn't have said he was a cinch, but he'da been one of the real contenders. But he couldn't beat a man in that heavy mud."

After the race, Shoemaker also said that Silky had trouble handling the track. "We were slippin' and slidin' all the way," Shoemaker said. "For a moment when he started moving up in the turn, I thought he might do it once he got straightened out in the stretch. Then he started slippin' and slidin' again, and I knew we were through."

Even in defeat, Silky was still worshipped by his exercise boy, Pete Kozar. "Nashua, Native Dancer, Man o' War, Joe Louis, Jack Dempsey, they all lost," Kozar said. "I still think Silky is great."

Which was more than Shoemaker said after he had more time to think about it. "All the publicity in the world couldn't have moved Silky up enough to win the Derby," Shoemaker said years later. "Silky wasn't a bad horse, but he wasn't a real good horse either. He didn't have the class to run with the good horses. In California he beat some mediocre horses and looked great doing it, but I said then that he couldn't spot a horse like Tim Tam 25 lengths and expect to beat him."

Arcaro didn't sing Silky's praises either. "He really wasn't a good horse," Arcaro said. "They were making a big thing out of it. But he had no class."

Thirty-five years after that Derby, McAnally would recall: "I thought deep down in my heart he really wasn't a Derby horse. He sure brought a lot of color and everything to the Derby, but I knew he wasn't a true mile-and-a-quarter horse. At a given distance, he was a good horse. He was a come-from-behind sprinter. In my opinion, at seven furlongs, he would have beaten a good horse."

Silky got another chance in the Triple Crown series, going to Baltimore where his fans held up signs that read, We Still Love You, Silky and Hooray for Silky. Some threw kisses to Silky before the Preakness. But he flopped again and struggled home eighth in the field of twelve.

Silky raced as a four-year-old before being retired with a record of twelve victories in twenty-seven starts and earnings of $157,700.

Years later, *The Blood-Horse* magazine looked back on his career and opined, in effect, that Silky would have teamed nicely with Redford and Newman in *The Sting*.

"He had the style, appearance, and name of a con man: Silky Sullivan," the magazine observed. "And he conned all that part of America that likes to have a sentimental bet on the Kentucky Derby into making him the 1958 winter book favorite. Silky had a little throat problem, or adrenaline problem, in that he could do nothing but gallop along the first part of a race until the juices began to flow. Somewhere around the half-mile pole, he would appear to drop about six inches, level out, and begin to run."

In retirement, Silky had as much appeal as ever. It became traditional for him to promenade at Golden Gate Fields on St. Patrick's Day to celebrate his birthday. Silky had put on weight around the middle, but he still looked like a million dollars. Dressed for the occasion, he appeared with his mane decorated with green and white fluff balls.

Over the years, Golden Gate varied its Silky promotions on St. Patrick's Day. Gimmicks included providing free admission to everybody named Sullivan or O'Sullivan, and giving away small Silky posters, buttons, and key rings. Moreover, Silky received a birthday cake, and a floral blanket was placed on his back. Ever young at heart, Silky was known to shake the blanket off, and before exiting, he would kick his heels in such a way that left the impression that he was acknowledging the fans' applause.

Silky also made an annual public apearance at Santa Anita Park on the day of the Santa Anita Derby. Once a ham, always a ham—and he held his head high, knowing that thousands were watching his every move. His ears pricked and his rump bouncing with each frisky step, he confidently pranced onto the track and looked around, nodding his head and occasionally kicking his heels up. The fans loved it.

At stud, Silky didn't make it as a successful sire, although he was the father of four stakes winners—Blazing Silk (who earned $163,364), Mr. Payne, Son of Silky, and Silk Ring.

Silky was purchased by San Francisco import-auto dealer Kjell Qvale in the '60s and was the star of his new owner's Green Oaks Stud Farm in California's Napa Valley. He attracted visitors to the farm and received Christmas cards from his faithful fans. Each year Green Oaks would have a party for its employees and their families, and Silky would take part in the fun. Silky would be brought to the parties and children would clamor to ride him. Silky never protested. Sometimes as many as four children would be put on Silky at once, and, like a perfect gentleman, he would walk around with them on his back.

Looking back on Silky, Qvale once recalled, "Through his life, he remained a very spirited but friendly and docile stallion with an obvious affinity for children. He loved kids and on several occasions at the farm I would put young children on his back, and he loved it!

"My secretary was another situation, however, and he got rid of her quickly."

Qvale added that Silky never bit, nor did he ever kick at anything except the crowds when he went on parade at Golden Gate and Santa Anita in his retirement years. Silky was still showing off in front of his fans, kicking his heels in the air in 1977, the last year of his life. "This was a pretty spectacular maneuver for a 22-year-old horse that weighed nearly 1,500 pounds," declared Qvale.

Qvale always remembered Silky's conformation and confidence. "He was a marvelous physical specimen and had a magnificent air about him."

In defense of Silky's record at stud, Qvale said. "He was never bred to an expensive mare but had some very good runners as well as a lot of hard-knocking runners."

Silky stayed at Green Oaks until the farm was sold. He then was moved to new quarters for the last part of his life—the stable area at the Alameda County Fairgrounds in Pleasanton, California, where he was under the care of trainer Emmett Campbell and his wife.

The legendary horse died in his sleep in November 1977. He was twenty-two. The night before he passed away, Mrs. Campbell fed Silky some hay and grain. "And he seemed perfectly all right," she said. "Then he just went to sleep and never awakened."

Silky was laid to rest in the infield at Golden Gate Fields.

A month and a half after Silky's death, Tom Ross, one of his co-owners during his racing days, passed away at the age of seventy-eight.

It was Ross who once best summed up Silky's days of glory.

"It was fun while it lasted," Ross said.

That it was. Fun . . . and a great show.

7

That Hundredth Derby Was Woody's Crowning Moment

W. C. ("WOODY") STEPHENS REMEMBERS HIS ROOTS.

Just ask the legendary trainer what Kentucky means to him, and he'll reply, "We'll put it this way: I was born there, and I came up there as just a real little poor country boy. And I went to a country school where a teacher taught from the primer through the eighth grade. And as I began to get a little bit older and my dad let me have a pony and ride him, I learned to *love* him—and love those horses. So then, I began to hear about the racetrack, about jockeys. I never thought about trainers. So then I learned to gallop horses . . . and then I was able to ride my first winner at Hialeah opening day of '31.

"Then, people have said, 'Woody, what was your biggest disappointment in racing?' I said, 'Because I wasn't a better race rider—because I came to be a race rider.'"

But just because he didn't measure up as a jockey, Stephens didn't give up on racing. "I said, 'I love the track—if I can't make it as a race rider, maybe I'll make it as a trainer.'

"And now they've said to me, 'What was your biggest thrill—ever?' I said, 'The hundredth Kentucky Derby in front of the home folks, down home, to win that hundredth running.' And I said, 'The five Belmonts are beautiful, but I can never forget the one back home, the hundredth Derby. I won it in front of the home folks. That was a mighty big afternoon. Princess Margaret handed me that trophy and I walked back headed to the press box and I said, 'This country boy come a *long* way.'"

Trainer W. C. ("Woody") Stephens has finished in the money with eight of his fourteen Kentucky Derby starters. His record in the Derby:

1949—Halt, fifth
1952—Blue Man, third
1954—Goyamo, fourth
1963—Never Bend, second
1974—Cannonade, first
     Judger, eighth
1978—Believe It, third

1983—Caveat, third
     Chumming, twelfth
1984—Swale, first
1985—Stephan's Odyssey, second
1987—Conquistarose, ninth
1988—Forty Niner, second
     Cefis, eighth

(Photo by Bill Straus, courtesy Keeneland Association)

A long way, indeed.

Woodford Cefis Stephens, a Stanton, Kentucky, native who was born September 1, 1913, has made quite a name for himself since his early days in Kentucky. "When I threw that hoe down that tobacco patch and run, I feel like I've come a long way," he said.

He went to New York as a head trainer in 1943 with his wife, Lucille—and "when we crossed that Hudson into New York, we had four hundred dollars, and I told Lucille I didn't know what might happen."

What happened was that Stephens established a record that made him one of the most successful, one of the most respected, one of the most popular trainers in the history of the sport. And although Woody went to New York to make the grade in the Big Apple, he has never forgotten his way back to ol' Kentucky.

He's come back home to win two renewals of the Kentucky Derby—with Cannonade for that memorable 100th running in 1974 and with Swale in 1984—and to finish second in the Churchill Downs classic three times—with Never Bend in 1963, with Stephan's Odyssey in 1985, and with Forty Niner in 1988. "I believe that jockeys and trainers would rather win the Kentucky Derby than any race in the world," Stephens said.

Stephens also has won the Kentucky Oaks a record five times, including three for the Cain Hoy Stable of Capt. Harry F. Guggenheim—Hidden Talent (a division in 1959), Make Sail (1960), and Sally Ship (1963). Stephens' other triumphs in the Oaks have come with White Star Line (1978) and Heavenly Cause (1981). Altogether, he has seventeen stakes victories at Churchill Downs.

Stephens is no stranger to the winner's circle at Keeneland Race Course either. He formerly held the record for the most stakes victories (nineteen) at the Lexington, Kentucky, track.

Stephens goes back a long way with Keeneland. His

"I won it, but who did I win it with?" asked trainer W. C. ("Woody") Stephens after he watched two fillies that he trained—Heavenly Cause (on the inside) and De La Rose—battle it out in the 1981 Kentucky Oaks. The photo-finish camera showed that Heavenly Cause, ridden by Laffit Pincay, Jr., won over De La Rose, with Pat Day up. Both fillies were champions. Heavenly Cause was the best two-year-old filly of 1980, and De La Rose was champion female grass horse of 1981. (© 1981 Churchill Downs Incorporated/Kinetic Corporation)

name was in the program as the trainer of a filly named Wise Dart in the first race on the track's inaugural card on October 15, 1936. His very first triumph as a trainer came at Keeneland on April 16, 1940, with Bronze Bugle, winner of a six-furlong claiming race that carried an $800 purse.

Stephens has won the Ashland a record four times (Tall Weeds in 1949, Jota Jota in 1957, Hidden Talent in 1959, and Sally Ship in 1963) and the Breeders' Futurity a record four times (Brother Tex in 1954, Harbor Springs in 1975, Swale in 1983, and Forty Niner in 1987).

In addition, he has triumphed in a record-equaling three runnings of the Blue Grass—Halt in 1949, Goyamo in 1954, and Judger in 1974.

Stephens points out that he actually saddled another Blue Grass winner—Our Boots in 1941—but Steve Judge was listed in the program as the colt's trainer. "In 1940, Our Boots won the Futurity in New York, and Mr. Judge came to me and asked me if I would go to work for him as assistant trainer and take Our Boots to Hot Springs and train him for the Kentucky Derby," Stephens recalled. "I took him, and my brother, Bill, who was 16, groomed him. I brought Our Boots back to Lexington, and Mr. Judge got pneumonia. Then I trained him for the Blue Grass, and he beat Whirlaway."

In 1975, Stephens won the first $100,000 race in Keeneland's history—the $130,725 Breeders' Futurity with Harbor Springs. Following that race, Stephens said with a smile: "As long as Kentucky keeps treating me this well, I'll keep coming back. I love coming to Kentucky."

Stephens has twice triumphed in the Queen Elizabeth II Challenge Cup at Keeneland, the first with Contredance in 1985 and then with Lotka in 1986. Recalling the latter race, Stephens said, "It was so funny that afternoon. Princess Alexandra presented the trophy, and she said, 'Woody, I bet a few bob on your filly.'"

Laughing, Stephens added: "I don't know *yet* what a bob is."

Stephens may not know what a bob is, but he certainly knows his racehorses. He started out at an early age with horses. His father, Lewis, was a farmer—"and he'd pitch me up on these mules' backs when he was plowing and I'd ride them. Then he bought me a pony when I was six years old. So it's been horses all my life."

Stephens named the pony Bill and trained him so well that he could ride him to the railroad track in Midway, Kentucky, and stand there when a train went past. J. M. Parrish, a local banker who had horses, was impressed with this trick and asked Stephens' father if the youngster would break his yearlings. "I was 13 that fall," Stephens said. "Mr. Parrish had three horses. I galloped those horses. The next year people began to notice me. I never dreamed of being a trainer. I came to be a rider. Sherrill Ward's father [John S. Ward] came to see my daddy and said, 'I'll take him to New York, and I'll tell you what I think when I bring him back.' So I went to New York with Mr. Ward, and when he come back he put a contract down in front of my dad and me. And I signed it for five years. I broke my maiden on a filly of his, Directly, at Hialeah in '31."

Directly, a three-year-old filly, carried 105 pounds. "That's how light I was," Stephens said.

"I rode a horse for Mr. Ward one day in Chicago in 1935, and I came back to the stable and he said, 'Woody, if you've got a future in racing, it'll be in trainin'—not ridin'—and if you want me to, I'll help you.' Mr. Ward was a wonderful man. He wanted to see me make it. He could have let me go, run me off, 'cause he didn't need me. But for some reason, he was *determined* to see that I made it."

Ward was so determined that when Keeneland launched its inaugural meeting in the fall of 1936, he saw to it that Stephens' name appeared in the program as the trainer of

Wise Dart. "He said, 'Woody, it might help you—go get your name on that program.'"

Wise Dart, owned by the Everglades Stable, was sent off at 7.60–1 odds in a field of eight juvenile fillies. The race, a six-furlong sprint, carried a $1,000 purse, but Wise Dart didn't get a piece of the money. The best she could do was a sixth-place finish.

Wise Dart may have lost that race, but Woody Stephens was off and running in the Thoroughbred business . . . and on his way to greatness. Ward's son, Sherrill, once paid Stephens the ultimate compliment. "I thought my father was a good horse trainer," he said, "but I think Woody's the best I ever saw."

No doubt about it, Stephens is a horseman's horseman, the highest praise any trainer can receive.

Stephens has done it all, and he's been honored accordingly.

In 1976, he was inducted into racing's Hall of Fame at Saratoga Springs, New York.

In 1983, he won the Eclipse Award as the country's top trainer.

In 1985, he was the honored guest of the Thoroughbred Club of America's annual testimonial dinner in Lexington, Kentucky. "It's a very nice thing to be recognized by this group of people, but to be their honored guest, well, that's just unbelievable," Stephens said at the time. "Very few trainers ever have had this honor, and I feel very, very fortunate. I have to keep pinching myself to see if it's really happening to me. This is something I really never dreamed of. And it's something I won't forget."

In 1986, he was honored at Churchill Downs with a Woody Stephens Day at the spring meeting, and that summer he was inducted into the Kentucky Athletic Hall of Fame.

His unprecedented streak of five straight Belmont Stakes victories is truly remarkable, a feat that ranks among the greatest in the history of all sports. He captured his first Belmont in 1982 with Conquistador Cielo, who went on to earn the Horse of the Year title that season, and then the veteran trainer sent out the following winners in "The Test of the Champion"—Caveat (a son of Cannonade) in 1983, Swale in 1984, Creme Fraiche in 1985, and Danzig Connection in 1986.

Stephens also has trained one Preakness winner (Blue Man in 1952).

Stephens trained his first stakes winner, Saguaro, in 1945 and has won stakes with more than one hundred horses.

In addition, Stephens has trained eleven champions, a record that stood until D. Wayne Lukas topped it in 1989. Stephens' eleven champions: Bald Eagle (1960 handicap horse), Bold Bidder (1966 handicap horse in one poll), Conquistador Cielo (1982 Horse of the Year and three-year-old colt), De La Rose (1981 female turf horse), Devil's Bag (1983 two-year-old colt), Forty Niner (1987 two-year-old colt), Heavenly Cause (1980 two-year-old filly), Never Bend (1962 two-year-old colt), Sensational (1976 two-year-old filly), Smart Angle (1979 two-year-old filly), and Swale (1984 three-year-old colt).

Stephens has won major races with two-year-olds and older horses, with sprinters and distance runners, with turf specialists and dirt stars. He has trained for many of the famous names in racing—Cain Hoy, Claiborne, John M. Olin, John Gaines, Henryk de Kwiatkowski, John Hanes, Hickory Tree, Ryehill, the Brady family, August Belmont, Brushwood Stable, Newstead, Woodvale Farm, and L. P. Doherty.

Asked to name the best horse he's ever trained, Stephens has been known to reply in this fashion: "I'm gonna put three of 'em down there. I'm gonna put Devil's Bag, Conquistador Cielo, and Bald Eagle. I'll tell you why: Conquistador won seven in a row. Bald Eagle is the only horse to win Internationals back to back. And, of course, Devil's Bag, you know what a 2-year-old he was. He never got beat and he never had a whip turned up on him as a 2-year-old. He was unbelievable. He was the best 2-year-old I ever trained."

Conquistador Cielo put his seven-race winning streak together during his 1982 Horse of the Year campaign. Those triumphs included the Metropolitan in a sizzling track-record mile of 1:33, a fourteen-length romp in the Belmont and an impressive four-length victory in the Dwyer.

Bald Eagle was sent to Europe early in his career and was trained there by Capt. Cecil Boyd-Rochfort, but the colt "was a disappointment," Stephens said. "So they decided after he got beat in the [Epsom] Derby and the Guineas to send him to me, and I started out with him, and all at once the horse began to turn around."

Bald Eagle, responding to Stephens' touch, captured the Washington, D.C., International in 1959 and 1960, the only horse to triumph two straight years in that prestigious race. He also won the 1960 Widener in 1:59³/₅ for the mile and one-quarter, a track record that stood for twenty-six years ("President Truman presented me the trophy," Stephens said) and also in 1960 captured the Metropolitan under 128 pounds in 1:33³/₅, a track record at the new Aqueduct.

As for Devil's Bag, the celebrated two-year-old champion of 1983 won all five of his starts that season, including a six-length score in the one-mile Champagne Stakes in a blazing 1:34¹/₅. Devil's Bag suffered his first loss in the 1974 Flamingo Stakes, finishing fourth. He later won the seven-furlong Forerunner Purse (by fifteen lengths) at Keeneland and the Derby Trial at Churchill Downs, but he didn't run in the Kentucky Derby and was retired with a record of eight victories in nine starts. Although Devil's Bag was on the sidelines on the first Saturday in May of

'84, Stephens won that Derby with Swale. "Swale was a great horse," Stephens said. "He died after the Belmont. We have no idea *why* it happened. The way he won the Derby and the way he won the Belmont, he was a great horse."

At the time that Swale won the Derby, Stephens was suffering from underlying emphysema complicated by pneumonia and a broken rib sustained in a bathroom accident in Florida. He was hospitalized for twelve days in Louisville that spring under the care of Dr. Dave Richardson, his second cousin.

Four days before the Derby, Stephens left his hospital in Louisville for a brief appearance at Churchill Downs to announce that Devil's Bag wouldn't be running in the Derby. Devil's Bag had won the Derby Trial the previous Saturday at the Downs, but the race was far from impressive. He won by 2¼ lengths over Biloxi Indian, who had lost to Devil's Bag by eighteen and nine lengths in the Champagne and Cowdin, respectively, the previous fall.

In a statement released from the hospital on Tuesday morning of Derby Week, Stephens said: "We missed a lot of valuable time with this horse when we shipped to New York and caught bad weather there. When we decided to come to Kentucky, we hoped the two shorter races, including the Derby Trial over the Churchill Downs track, would be enough to get this horse ready for the Derby. While I could not criticize the horse's race Saturday, he did get very tired. He backed off a bit on Sunday, and, despite the fact that he looks real bright now, I have decided not to run him. I think I have a powerful horse in Swale, who has a big chance to win the Derby."

As it turned out, Devil's Bag never raced again. Two days after the Derby, it was announced that X rays revealed a small chip in his right knee and that he would be retired.

Swale, sired by 1977 Triple Crown champion Seattle Slew, came into the Derby off a bad second-place finish in the Lexington Stakes at Keeneland. Sent off as the overwhelming favorite in the Lexington, Swale was beaten eight lengths by He Is a Great Deal on a sloppy track. "I'm going to take my chance with Swale," Stephens said. "If he runs back to his Gulfstream race [a victory in the Florida Derby], he'll run a good race. Just throw out the race in Lexington in the slop."

Stephens left the hospital two days before the Derby and stayed in the Executive Inn. Churchill Downs president Lynn Stone arranged for a limousine to bring Stephens to the track on both Oaks and Derby days. Miss Oceana, trained by Stephens, rallied from last place in the Oaks and just missed catching Lucky Lucky Lucky, who triumphed by a nose.

On Derby Day, Stephens didn't look like himself at the track. He was weak, his cheeks were drawn, and his color was ashen. But the day came up roses for Stephens and Swale. Viewing the Derby on television in the directors' room at the Downs, Stephens watched Swale take the lead and declared, "He's going to win by five."

Swale won by 3¼ lengths but no doubt could have triumphed by five if jockey Laffit Pincay, Jr., had pushed him. Swale was that much the best in that '84 Derby.

Stephens bet $400 to win on Swale, and Richardson made $1,600 in win wagers on the colt. Swale paid $8.80 on a $2-win bet, so Stephens collected $1,760 (a $1,360 profit), and Richardson walked away with $7,040 (a $5,440 profit).

Just as Swale was considered a second-stringer to Devil's Bag, Stephens' other Derby winner, Cannonade, was rated No. 2 to Judger, the favorite who finished eighth in the '74 Run for the Roses after breaking from the No. 22 post position and encountering traffic problems.

Afterward, Stephens was asked why the better horse in his entry didn't win. "I never did tell anybody he [Judger] was the better horse," Stephens said. "I've always thought that the only edge Cannonade had was he had raced over the racetrack and we knew he'd like it. I just don't think Judger got ahold of this track and didn't run his best."

Cannonade was owned by John M. Olin and Judger by Seth Hancock. Leading up to the '74 Derby, Stephens said: "I train both of them the best I know how, and I'm sure both owners know that. I'll give orders to riders to ride each horse individually to his best. I'll run Cannonade like the other one isn't in there. And I'll run Judger the same way. These horses have been so close together."

In the Florida Derby, Judger won and Cannonade came in second, beaten by three-quarters of a length. "Pete Anderson did get criticism that he used Cannonade a lot," Stephens said, "and he didn't do it with me telling him to. He just called his shot, and a lot of people thought he called it a little quick when he moved at the five-eighths pole. But then Cannonade still fought back. He's a dead game horse."

Another entry in the '74 Derby—Rube the Great and Accipiter, owned by Sigmund Sommer—was once trained by Stephens, who sold those two, along with the filly, Tourniquette, in a three-horse deal for $200,000 in the fall of 1973. While racing for Stephens, the horses were owned by the Brady family's stable, Mill House.

"We discussed the risk that we were taking—you know, selling young horses before they had raced much," Stephens said before the Derby. "But I felt that we put a good price on the horse—all you could ask at that time."

Stephens had started Rube the Great and Accipiter five times each before they were sold to Sommer.

In a later interview, Stephens said: "It was a funny feeling in the 1974 Derby—the first four horses that walked on the racetrack, if I hadn't sold those two [Rube the Great and Accipiter], it's a possibility that I would have run a four-horse entry. Now wouldn't that have been something? But I probably wouldn't have run the two that I beat.

"This is awfully funny: When I walked in the paddock to saddle my entry, Sig Sommer was standing there and he said, 'Woody, are you nervous?' And I said, 'Naw, Sig, because I have you in my pocket. You belong to me today.' He said, 'Well, I'm not nervous either, but I'm a little bit drunk.'

"I just thought my horses were were better all along anyhow," Stephens added. "That day, my horse fired, and his horses didn't. I felt that that would have been a terrible thing if I should have sold the Derby winner. After that, I didn't care, but that day I didn't want him to beat me."

Rube the Great and Accipiter were both stabled in Barn 42 at the Downs, the same barn in which Cannonade and Judger resided.

The day after that Derby, a grinning Stephens said of Rube the Great and Accipiter: "If they had beat me, it would have been time for Woody Stephens to retire. I did think they were nice horses and I sold them at a good price to a lovely man, but I just didn't think they would beat the two that I kept. Some people were preaching Rube the Great, but Rube the Great beat claimers."

Cannonade, a son of Bold Bidder, started in three races at Churchill Downs and won each time. He captured the 1973 Kentucky Jockey Club Stakes by $2\frac{1}{2}$ lengths, and a week before the '74 Derby he came home two lengths on top in the Stepping Stone Purse. Then in the Derby, he made it three for three at the Downs, triumphing by $2\frac{1}{4}$ lengths.

"When I won the Jockey Club Stakes in the fall," Stephens recalled, "I said to Lynn Stone, 'Lynn, I'll be back the first Saturday in May.' And *there he was*. He ran big. He did love the track."

Cannonade provided Stephens with such a great thrill in the Derby, but the trainer has many other fond recollections on the racetrack, including the 1988 Travers won by Forty Niner. "That was one of the gamest races I ever saw in my life," Stephens said. "Forty Niner fought back. I never will forget that morning Chris McCarron come in the tack room to talk to me. I always liked Chris. I think he's as good a rider as there is in the world. I said, 'Chris, this horse, in my opinion, has got a big kick about five-sixteenths of a mile. I believe that Pat [Day] could have moved a little late on him in the Kentucky Derby. But I'd like to see you sit off this pace about three lengths until you're coming to the five-sixteenth pole—then move, 'cause he's got a big kick. Turning for home, I want him in front, and when you put him on the lead turning for home, shut the gate. Let *nobody* in there.' And Pat Day was starting in there on the inside on [Ogden] Phipps' horse [Seeking the Gold], and they fought it out from there to the wire, and I beat him a nose. But you talk about fight-back—and he didn't only do it one time, he did it a lot of times. I just thought he got a perfect ride that day from McCarron.

"Forty Niner got beat a neck in the Kentucky Derby, and he had [the] No. 17 post. He might have been the best horse, I don't know. I thought he was going to make it at the sixteenth pole, but he didn't, and I've always wondered if maybe Pat waited a little late to move or else he got there and hung on the money or the filly come again to beat me. She beat me a neck, Winning Colors. But there's no question about it, he was a *good* racehorse."

Forty Niner was second the first time past the wire in that Derby, then dropped back to third and later fourth going down the backstretch before launching a stretch rally that fell short.

Stephens also trained Danzig, a talented colt whose career was cut short by injury. Danzig, who raced for Henryk de Kwiatkowski, won his three lifetime starts (in 1979 and 1980) by a total of 21¾ lengths. "No horse ever put his nose in front of him," Stephens noted.

"I bought Danzig for $310,000 at Saratoga," Stephens said. "He had a big splint, but I looked at it so close and I had a feeling it never would hurt him."

The splint, Stephens believes, discouraged some buyers from bidding on Danzig, a son of Northern Dancer. "You don't buy Northern Dancer horses for $310,000," Stephens said. "I liked this horse, except that big knot on his shin. So I got in there and I bid on him and I stole him—$310,000. Then I put him away and broke him. Then I sent him to Aiken, South Carolina, that winter with my brother, Bill, and that splint practically went away completely. And it went away till you didn't know it was there.

"The first time I started him, he won by 8½ lengths. But he come up with a darn chip in his knee, and I sent him to Dr. [Bob] Copelan in Kentucky to take it out. We took it out and give him a lot of time, but when he come back it still wasn't right. I went along training him, and by being awful careful, I got him to the races. He won off big. I was watching that knee so careful, and then I ran him back. Then I nominated him for a stake, so I worked him a mile, and he went his first half in 53 or 54, his last half in 47 seconds. You don't find horses who do those things. I X-rayed him again after that work, and I sent the pictures to Copelan. He said, 'Woody, you're going to destroy this horse.' I said, 'Doctor, I'm not going to destroy him 'cause he'll never run again. This is *it*.' Henryk was in Europe, so I called him and told him that I decided to stop the horse. Well, he let me do what I wanted to do. I told him, 'To me, I not only think Claiborne Farm is the best farm in America, I think it's probably as good as there is in the world and I'd just love to see this horse go there.' And I was friendly with Seth [Claiborne president Seth Hancock]. I had Judger for him.

"So I asked Seth to take him. He said. 'Woody, how am I going to do any good with a horse that's started three times in his life and never run in a stake in his life?' I said, 'Seth, I can't help what he's done or what he hasn't done. All I know is he's a running horse. Just syndicate him any price that you can put on him and take this horse 'cause I don't believe ever I had a horse could do what this horse could do.' So now he's at Claiborne, and Seth syndicated him. He's just as good a sire, I think, as there is in the country. I'm so high on that horse. Right now he's just doing nothing but good, and he's getting good mares."

Danzig, who ranked as the leading North American sire by progeny earnings in 1991, 1992, and 1993, has been represented by many standout runners, including Contredance and Lotka, the two fillies who won the Queen Elizabeth II Challenge Cup, and Stephan's Odyssey and Chief's Crown, the two-three finishers in the 1985 Kentucky Derby. Danzig also sired Danzig Connection, the last of Stephens' five Belmont winners. That '86 Belmont gave Stephens particular pleasure. In triumphing in that race, Stephens beat out two older trainers—Walter Kelley, who sent out runner-up Johns Treasure, and Charlie Whittingham, the conditioner of third-place finisher Ferdinand.

"I told Charlie when he came for the Belmont, I said, 'Now, Charlie, when you cross that Hudson, these buildings get really tall.' He said, 'Woody, I'm not comin' in a covered wagon.' Isn't that beautiful?"

Stephens couldn't resist one parting shot at that time about getting the best of Kelly and Whittingham in that Belmont. "Those two dirty old men—Kelly's 79 and Charlie's 73—they tried to beat me in my town," he said. "They tried to wipe me out! They must be crazy!"

And Stephens cackled.

Looking back on his career, Stephens said, "I've been lucky enough to win just so many, with Guggenheim, with this one, with that one. I've never thought I did it better

Hall of Fame trainers W. C. ("Woody") Stephens (right) and Charlie Whittingham at Arlington Park in 1986. (Photo by Jim Bolus)

than anyone else, but now I do feel like I am a pro. I don't mean trainin' horses, but I've learned how to get along with people—owners, trainers, media, everybody—and I think that's awful big in this game."

Throughout his career, Stephens has demonstrated patience—with horses and people alike. Trainer Billy Badgett, who formerly worked under Stephens, told Eclipse Award-winning writer Jack Mann: "I have never, ever heard the man raise his voice, and that is unbelievable. He has ways of getting around things, handling them with such professionalism. He never acts like a know-it-all, though he'd certainly have a right to."

Stephens has carved out such a distinguished career that his autobiography, *Guess I'm Lucky*, was published in 1985. If there's anything that the good-natured Stephens does as well as train horses, it's tell stories, and he likes to recall the time in 1986 when he was at Suffolk Downs autographing his book. "When I was signing these books, they said, 'Woody, has there ever been a mention of a movie of the story of your life?' I said, 'I'm gonna let 'em do it as long as they'll let Dolly Parton play the part of Lucille.' Lucille said, 'Now, that isn't nice.'"

Stephens cackled.

"I've been lucky enough to have a great wife," he said. "Lucille and I both feel this way: If we have a horse that made us a million dollars or made us a dollar, it didn't change our life. Lucille's the same girl she was a long time ago. We might try to buy nicer clothes or something. Anything we want, we try to get. But as far as the same friends, if she finds out one of her friends—those girls she went to high school with—is sick or something, she'll try to send her flowers or call. And that's the life we've tried to live."

Stephens, who grew up in Midway, Kentucky, was honored with a Woody Stephens Day in that town in 1989. Also in 1989, Powell County honored Stephens, a native son, by unveiling a bronze bust of him and Forty Niner.

The bust was dedicated at the courthouse in Stanton, Kentucky.

"I like Kentucky," Stephens said in March of 1990. "Here's the way I feel: At my age and all, if ever I do quit, Kentucky's the right place for me for this reason: There's a lot of racing through Kentucky and sales going on all the time. It would give me something to do. And I have five mares at Claiborne, and I could go out there and see my foals. So if ever I do quit, I'll buy a place back in Lexington."

A couple of months later, Stephens underwent quadruple-bypass heart surgery in Louisville. During the summer of 1990, Stephens commented on his illness, saying: "I laid in that bed three months. It was a rough go. I don't think the doctors thought I was going to make it."

But Stephens remarkably came through the surgery and the long recovery.

One of these days, it would seem only appropriate for W. C. ("Woody") Stephens to return to the Bluegrass State. After all, he's always felt right at home in ol' Kentucky.

As he once put it, "Kentucky's where I'm from, and Kentucky someday is where I'll go back. And I will."

Don DeWitt. (Photo by Jim Bolus)

Dan Farley.

Cliff Guilliams. (Photo by Jim Bolus)

Russ Harris.

8

Looking for the Derby Winner? Well, Listen Up

AT KENTUCKY DERBY TIME, all you have to do is listen and you'll hear plenty of tips on the big race.

The trick is to know whose tip to follow.

Pointing to the Derby Winner

Don DeWitt, one of the most knowledgeable and astute handicappers in the business, is a Louisvillian who has followed the Derby for years. His selections have appeared for nineteen years in the *Louisville Daily Sports News*, popularly known around town as "the finger sheet," and for the 1990 Derby his picks were in the *Kentucky Inter-Track News*.

In "the finger sheet," DeWitt's pick in each race is designated by the form of a finger pointing to the horse he has selected. On Derby Day in 1986, the finger was alongside the name of Ferdinand, with the following comment from DeWitt: "Strong as a bull in the final quarter-mile." Which is exactly what Ferdinand was.

In 1987, the finger pointed to Alysheba, with DeWitt commenting: "Bluegrass bid put him on the muscle." Indeed, Alysheba's effort in the Blue Grass Stakes—a first-place finish although he was disqualified—set him up just right for his Derby victory.

When he tabbed Ferdinand and Alysheba, DeWitt provided his readers with horses who were nice prices. Ferdinand went off at 17.70–1, Alysheba at 8.40–1.

In 1989, DeWitt was undecided between Sunday Silence and Western Playboy. He flipped a coin, and it came up Western Playboy, who came in last. Sunday Silence won.

In 1990, DeWitt picked Unbridled, a 10.80–1 risk, in the *Kentucky Inter-Track News*. DeWitt's pre-race comment: "Unbridled will be unsaddled in circle."

And in 1993, those bettors who were wise enough to call DeWitt on a 900 number received a tip on Sea Hero, who won the Derby at odds of 12.90–1.

Two in a Row for Dandy Dan

Dan Farley is another who gives his readers horses at healthy prices.

Writing for *Racing Post*, a publication based in London, England, Farley picked two straight long shots in 1992 and 1993—Lil E. Tee at 16.80–1 and then Sea Hero.

In the 1992 Derby, he dared to pick against Arazi, the celebrated European-based runner who finished eighth as the 9–10 favorite.

"Arazi first, the rest nowhere? Maybe, since even the vast majority of the American side see little hope for the home team, including second choice A. P. Indy. But I go against the prevailing view and choose Lil E. Tee.

"Trainer Lynn Whiting saddles a consistently high percentage of winners. No braggart, he seldom talks up any of his runners, but in Lil E. Tee he sees a horse with a very good chance for victory—and he says so.

"Jockey Pat Day has been expected to win a Kentucky Derby for years, but has experienced considerable disappointment. What a perfect time to achieve a Derby victory, when no one is looking.

"And Lil E. Tee himself has points in his favour. He drew the [No.] 10 post, the perfect spot for a rider as brilliant on the lead as Day to use the colt's tactical speed. He'll get the trip—his sire was a solid third in the 1984

Lil E. Tee, winner of the 1992 Kentucky Derby. (Photo by Jim Bolus)

Sea Hero, winner of the 1993 Kentucky Derby. (Photo by Jim Bolus)

Derby. And he is coming to the race as well as any of his rivals.

"Let's make it Lil E. Tee over Arazi, A. P. Indy, and Dr Devious. And if it really is Arazi first, the rest nowhere, we'll sit back and enjoy that one, too."

On Derby Day in 1993, readers of *Racing Post* came across this headline: Sea became a hero."

Farley wrote: "Today's Kentucky Derby at Churchill Downs is a jigsaw puzzle—and none of the pieces seem to fall together with ease.

"The 10-furlong Classic has an obvious favourite in Prairie Bayou, but my fancy is Paul Mellon's Sea Hero, a 40–1 shot on the morning line. He is winless since gaining a smashing victory in the Champagne Stakes at Belmont Park last autumn, but there's an explanation for that.

"Sent to Florida for the Breeders' Cup, he was well beaten, and lost his next two starts in that state as well, but trainer Mack Miller is sure the colt did not appreciate the climate there.

"Sea Hero awakened with a good effort in the nine-furlong, Grade 2 Blue Grass Stakes at Keeneland last time out, going down by just short of three lengths to Prairie Bayou while not at his best.

"He can surely get the Derby distance given his pedigree (Polish Navy–Glowing Tribute, by Graustark), and he has come on perhaps better than any other Derby starter during the week."

Not only did Farley pick the '93 Derby winner, but he selected Prairie Bayou to run second. The Sea Hero-Prairie Bayou exacta paid $190.60.

Guilliams: Always on Target

Cliff Guilliams is the *Daily Racing Form* chart caller at the Kentucky tracks. A keen observer, he doesn't miss anything on the racetrack, and when it comes to picking the Derby, he's one of the best.

In the fall of 1983, while covering racing for the *Evansville Courier*, Guilliams liked Swale so much after watching the colt win the Breeders' Futurity that he picked him to win the 1984 Derby. In a story appearing on Derby Day, Guilliams wrote: "Last fall when I watched Swale win the Breeders' Futurity at Keeneland, I said I thought he could win the Kentucky Derby. I'll stick to my guns. For his entire career, until today, Swale has been in the shadow of his touted stablemate, Devil's Bag, who was withdrawn from Derby contention Tuesday by trainer Woody Stephens. Although Swale was upset by He Is a Great Deal in the Lexington Stakes at Keeneland, I still believe he has what it takes to win. What he needs is a fast track and the same gallant effort he exhibited in the Florida Derby when he held off Dr. Carter the length of the stretch."

The track was fast for the 1984 Derby, and Swale won by $3\frac{1}{4}$ lengths.

In 1990, Guilliams correctly picked the first two Derby finishers—Unbridled and Summer Squall.

Guilliams didn't get carried away by all of the Arazi hype. Following Arazi's sensational five-length victory in the 1991 Breeders' Cup Juvenile, some people were ready to concede the 1992 Derby to this colt. However, in the Churchill Downs press box shortly after the Breeders' Cup, Guilliams said, "Arazi won today against this field. The Derby is a long way off—and it's not at a mile and a sixteenth, either."

Guilliams was right again.

A Serious Student All the Way Around

Russ Harris is not just a serious student of handicapping. He's a serious student. He earned his bachelor's degree in journalism and political science from Kent State in

1949. In 1954, he received his master's degree in government from New York University (with a 4.0 average), and thirty-nine years later—in 1993—he obtained his second master's degree, this one in history from Villanova, again with a 4.0 average.

Not many writers can say that they also have served as a steward, but Harris can. He was a steward at Arlington Park and Washington Park in 1963, 1964, and 1965 and at Hawthorne in 1964, 1965, and 1966.

Harris covered twenty runnings of the Derby, the first in 1966 for *Newsday*, then for the *Philadelphia Inquirer* and *New York Daily News*.

Harris just may be the world's best handicapper, but take it from him, picking the Derby winner can be difficult. "I have to admit right off the bat that I am not the best Derby handicapper," he said. "In my opinion, it's usually a race where your mother-in-law could out-handicap you without even knowing how to read the *Racing Form*. I think it's the distance of the race so early in the year that makes it so tough."

Not that he has come up empty in picking the Derby. Harris takes his business seriously, and he isn't one to stab at a long shot just for the glory of picking an outsider. He selects horses for all the right reasons, and over the years he's picked his share of Derby winners, including Cannonade, considered the lesser half of an entry with Judger, in 1974.

And two years later, he went with Bold Forbes, who upset Honest Pleasure. "It gave me—as I wrote—the most honest pleasure I had enjoyed in Louisville up to that date," Harris declared.

Honest Pleasure went off as the 2–5 favorite, and Bold Forbes was the 3–1 second choice. In analyzing that Derby, he recalled: "Both of these colts were speed horses, but some longtime observers thought Honest Pleasure was pounds the best of that year's crop. I used a pre-race quote from Bud Lyon, the veteran *Daily Racing Form* chart caller. He said of Honest Pleasure [who was 4-for-4 as a three-year-old]: 'I'll be amazed if he doesn't make a shambles of this field. He may be the best horse I've ever seen." [Bud was a good friend of LeRoy Jolley, trainer of Honest Pleasure.]

"I was on very friendly terms with both Braulio Baeza, rider of Honest Pleasure, and Angel Cordero, Jr., rider of Bold Forbes. Usually, jockeys are the last to know anything about handicapping horses, but that wasn't the point here. If you know Cordero, you know he was a daring rider, always willing to take a chance and *move early* if need be, whatever it took to get an edge. Baeza, on the other hand, was cool and cautious; the one thing Braulio never did on a horse was to move too soon. There was no way he would *send* Honest Pleasure early and get him cooked in a speed duel. [He did just that in the Preakness, but that was on Jolley's orders and was based on what happened in Kentucky.]

"Cordero opened up five on the first turn, and when Honest Pleasure challenged in the stretch, Bold Forbes had enough left to win by a length.

"They were one-two all the way around, and Elocutionist, who was to benefit from a speed duel and win the Preakness, finished a remote third.

"I think this Derby was one of the few in which knowing the personality and style of the riders paid off and one which also revealed the debits of a speed horse. It's hard to win the Derby on the front end in any event, but almost impossible when there are two horses with major speed in the field. If Baeza had challenged Cordero early, Elocutionist might well have won the Derby as well as the Preakness."

Ruby: All Alone with Ponder

Earl Ruby, sports editor of *The Courier-Journal*, had a special knack at picking the Derby winner.

In 1949, he was the only one of eighty-six writers polled by *The Courier-Journal* to pick the Derby winner, Ponder, a 16–1 long shot.

Larry Boeck of *The Courier-Journal* wrote: "Ruby's daring choice of Ponder was no wild guess or penchant to be different. He had good reasons."

Ruby was quoted as saying: "The way Ben Jones [trainer of Ponder] made it his business to tout the experts off Ponder gave me the idea that maybe Ponder was his ace in the hole, after all. Jones was talking low before the race, and maybe he had something there . . . if the other jockeys don't think your horse will give them trouble they're apt not to pay much attention to him. Then he can slip through.

"Then the way Ponder finished in the Derby Trial, steaming in the stretch to almost catch Olympia, cinched him as a winner in my mind."

In 1950, Ruby and two other writers—Red Smith of the *New York Herald Tribune* and Arthur Daley of *The New York Times*—correctly picked the 1–2–3 Derby finshers—Middleground, Hill Prince, and Mr. Trouble. And in 1963 Ruby and Milt Dunnell of the *Toronto Daily Star* were the only two journalists to pick Derby winner Chateaugay, a 9.40–1 shot.

Eagle and Roesler Picked the Winner *and* the Time

As if picking the Derby winner isn't difficult enough, try hitting on the exact time of the race as well.

In 1964, sports editor Dean Eagle of *The Louisville Times* provided this tip to his readers: ". . . it's Northern Dancer by a nose over Hill Rise with Quadrangle third and The Scoundrel fourth. The time—a record two minutes flat."

Eagle also wrote: "I'm picking The Dancer because Bill Hartack seems to have better luck in the Derby than Willie Shoemaker." He also noted: "A fast mile in the Derby Trial might have taken some edge off Hill Rise, even though he appeared to be running easily."

That same year Bob Roesler, sports editor of *The Times-Picayune* in New Orleans, covered his first Derby and led off his story on the day of the race with this bold prediction: "Northern Dancer is going to win the Kentucky Derby by covering the mile and a quarter in the record-breaking time of two minutes flat. Hill Rise, the 6-to-5 favorite, will have to settle for second-place money with Quadrangle and Wil Rad the next under the wire in the 90th running of America's most glamorous horse race."

A bit farther down in his story, Roesler wrote: "Why pick the Dancer over Hill Rise?

"There are many reasons. First, I believe Horatio Luro has planned and carried out the Dancer's training perfectly. Luro himself admits he hasn't wanted to 'squeeze the lemon dry' in previous races. He has been saving most of the 'juice' for one occasion—the Kentucky Derby.

"Another reason for liking the Dancer is a brash young man named Bill 'Don't call me Willie' Hartack who took over when Willie Shoemaker decided to use Hill Rise for transportation in the Derby.

"Hartack has a better Derby 'batting average' than Shoe. Hartack has won with Decidedly (trained, incidentally, by Luro), Venetian Way, and Iron Liege in his five shots at the roses. The Shoe won with Tomy Lee and Swaps in 12 shots at the big race. . . .

"One big thing we feel Northern Dancer has going for him is his nimbleness. He therefore is less likely to get into trouble. And trouble often kills off a contender.

"Hill Rise is a long-striding colt and can not afford to get knocked off stride. On the other hand we've been told the Dancer can stop and start more quickly.

"It should be one heck of an exciting race."

The 1964 Derby was just that—one heck of an exciting race.

And Eagle and Roesler wrote about it beforehand as if they were looking into a crystal ball.

The nimble Northern Dancer, brilliantly ridden by Hartack, won by a neck over Hill Rise in track-record time of two minutes flat.

When it comes to picking the Kentucky Derby, it doesn't get much better than the job Dean Eagle and Bob Roesler did in 1964.

Play It Again, Sam

As sports editor of *The Courier-Journal*, Sam H. McMeekin gave his readers the winner of the 1919 Derby, Sir Barton, in his story the morning of the race. He also gave them a lead in his account of the Derby that he had used . . . and used.

In 1916, McMeekin led off his Derby story in this fashion:

"George Smith won the Derby!

"Like a frightened deer endeavoring to shake off a savage hound, straining to the bursting point every muscle of his aching body, this black son of Out of Reach—Consuelo II swept past the finish the winner by a scant neck over Star Hawk and gained for his owner, John Sanford, the Eastern sportsman, a princely sum."

Ol' Sam must have liked that lead, because the next year he wrote:

"An imported colt won the Derby!

"Like a hare unbrushed by savage hounds, Omar Khayyam, a chestnut son of Marco—Lisma, darted from his field at the eighth pole and swept under the wire winner by two lengths of the premier turf event of the Western Hemisphere, and gained a small fortune for his owners, C. K. G. Billings and Frederick Johnson, of New York."

Guess how Sammy Boy led off his account of the 1919 classic?

"Sir Barton won the Derby!

"Like a hare unbrushed by savage hounds, the chestnut son of Star Shoot–Lady Sterling darted from his field as the barrier was sprung and led to the end of this premier turf event of the Western Hemisphere. He gained for his owner, Commander J. K. L. Ross, the Canadian sportsman, a princely stake."

In 1920, McMeekin altered his lead somewhat—but not enough.

"He was bred in old Kentucky!

"From Hamburg Place, whence came Sir Barton and other stars, came yet another that yesterday inscribed his name in turf's hall of fame. Despised and ignored, the 'weak sister' of his stable, Paul Jones, a homely son of Sea King—May Florence, won the Kentucky Derby and gained for his owner, Ral Parr, the Baltimore sportsman, a princely sum.

"Like a gazelle disturbed by beasts of prey, Paul Jones darted from his field as the barrier was sprung and led to the end of the premier turf event of the Western Hemisphere."

If McMeekin had been around to cover the 1993 Run for the Roses, he likely would have reached into his bag of original leads and come out with the following:

"Sea Hero won the Derby!

"Like a hare unbrushed by savage hounds, the bay son of Polish Navy–Glowing Tribute darted from his field in the upper stretch and won the premier turf event of the Western Hemisphere. He gained for his owner, Paul Mellon, the Virginia sportsman, a princely stake."

It's 110 yards—about the length of a football field—from the six-teenth pole to the finish line. Over the years, jockeys have sometimes misjudged the Churchill Downs' finish line and stood up at the six-teenth pole. (Photos by Jim Bolus)

9

Misjudging That Derby Finish

FOOTBALL PLAYERS HAVE RUN the wrong way for touch-downs . . . basketball players have scored goals for opponents . . . and baseball players have wound up on bases already occupied by a teammate.

But when it comes down to embarrassing situations, when it comes right down to silly mistakes, no sport has anything on horse racing.

Jockeys, including some of racing's all-time greats, have committed major boo-boos by misjudging finish lines.

According to *Daily Racing Form* charts, it's happened at least four times in the Kentucky Derby, including Bill Shoemaker's stand-up routine on Gallant Man in 1957. Other jockeys to stand up prematurely in the Derby have been Job Dean Jessop, Sandy Hawley, and Jean Cruguet. (Cruguet, however, denies that he misjudged the finish line.) In addition, Willie ("Smokey") Saunders said that he almost pulled Omaha up in the 1935 Derby, although indications are that he may not have recalled the stretch run of that race exactly the way it happened.

When you consider that the Derby has been run 119 times, four misjudged finishes figure out to one in every thirty races. It's a good bet that if you went to any track in America, you wouldn't see a single jockey misjudge the finish line once in *three hundred* races, no less thirty. But in the Derby it's happened more times than you would expect.

Why is that?

It's anybody's guess.

You would think that in a race with the Derby's magnitude jockeys would know where the finish line is and would ride to the very end of the race.

There's no legitimate excuse for jockeys to misjudge the finish line. If they do so, they're guilty of carelessness. However, at Churchill Downs certain physical features might lead to that carelessness.

For one thing, the Downs stretch is a long one—all of 1,234½ feet from the last turn to the finish line. A jockey who might not be concentrating could make the mistake of thinking the race *should* be over by the time he arrives at the sixteenth pole, which is located a sixteenth of a mile before the finish line.

Nowadays, the sixteenth pole, which stands about ten feet tall, is white and edged in black. The finish pole is white topped by a ball painted in metal flake gold. This pole is about twenty-five feet tall and printed on it in big letters—and in English—is the word *Finish*. Hard to miss, that finish pole.

But just twelve yards or so after the horses pass the sixteenth pole, the paddock runway is to the right. And then just a bit farther down the track a jockey can notice to his left the Derby winner's circle and the infield pagoda, all of which might lead the rider to think he's at the finish of the race.

Then, even farther down the stretch is the finish pole standing tall for every rider to see. But sometimes riders don't see this pole in time and they stand up prematurely, thinking the race is over.

Let's take a look at the misjudged finishes in the Derby—and in certain other races at the Downs as well.

A Nightmare Finish for Shoe

During the week of the 1957 Derby, owner Ralph Lowe had a dream. He dreamed that his colt, Gallant Man, was charging down the stretch in the Derby, on his way to certain victory, when his rider suddenly misjudged the finish line and pulled up prematurely, costing his horse the race.

Shoemaker, informed of the dream, told Lowe not to worry. And then Shoemaker went out and stood up at the sixteenth pole aboard the surging Gallant Man, who lost by a nose to Iron Liege.

"I didn't pull him up when I eased up in the saddle, but the change in my position caused him to hesitate momentarily—just enough that we dropped from a nose to a head behind," Shoemaker later explained. "He didn't break stride, though."

Steward Lincoln Plaut, who alertly spotted the incident, thought it "undoubtedly" cost Gallant Man the race. "I think Gallant Man had to win by at least a length if Shoemaker doesn't make that mistake," said Plaut. "You know he was going to win it in another jump anyhow."

Daily Racing Form chart caller Don Fair likewise was satisfied that Shoemaker's actions at the sixteenth pole cost Gallant Man the race. "It threw the horse off stride," Fair said, "and he was barely beat when he come up again."

Fair came in for considerable credit for noting the incident in the *Form*'s chart. But certain insiders have always contended that Fair didn't actually spot Shoemaker's standing up but instead was tipped off soon after the Derby by Plaut, himself once a chart caller. Fair denied that charge, saying: "There's no truth to that. I saw it myself."

Whether Fair saw the incident is open to debate. What likely isn't open to debate is whether any turf writer or sports columnist in the press box saw it. Most of them wouldn't have noticed it because their eyes weren't trained to spot such things or they simply weren't knowledgeable enough to know what they were seeing. If a *single* one had seen it, it's highly unlikely that he would have kept it to himself. He would have wanted confirmation from somebody else, and thus word would have spread like wildfire throughout the press box and the media would have bombarded Shoemaker with questions in the jockeys' room. As it was, Johnny Carrico of *The Courier-Journal* wrote afterward: "Willie Shoemaker, who had trouble locating the finish line with Gallant Man, was up to his usual silent self. He showered quickly and headed for the airport, making no mention of his classic error."

And Arthur Daley of *The New York Times* wrote: "Perhaps the most extraordinary part of the jockey room ceremonies was that Willie Shoemaker, the rider of Gallant Man, never mentioned to anyone what he'd told the stewards. Willie the Shoe told them that he'd misjudged the whereabouts of the finish line. And he didn't mention it again."

This quote was obtained from Shoemaker afterward: "I stood up for an instant, then realized my error and went back to work. I had to get after him at the five-eighths pole. I dug into him good, and the way we were moving, I thought I had it won. He's a good-trying horse. However, there wasn't any question in my mind that we were second; I didn't need the camera to tell me that."

Daley described just how quickly the incident happened: "Shoemaker realized his error the very instant he started to stand. He plopped back with the hasty embarrassment of the guest at the formal dinner who thinks he's being introduced by the toastmaster and discovers it's some other guy."

In his book entitled *Shoemaker*, the world's winningest jockey said he didn't make any excuses in '57 for what he did in the Derby. "Gallant Man might have hung a little, but I didn't cop a plea the day I made the mistake and I'm not doing it now." Shoemaker said.

H. A. ("Jimmy") Jones, the trainer of Iron Liege, didn't believe that Shoemaker's stand-up routine at the sixteenth pole had a bearing on the outcome of the race. "I don't think it was that important," Jones said. "I think it was way overplayed by everybody. Shoemaker raised his head up and right down again. But, of course, taking a moving picture, you can take that one frame and make him look like he's the Statue of Libery, you know. But he just raised up and went right down and went to riding. Nothing changed. Never changed anything. He just kept banging away. I asked Shoemaker at the time, 'Do you think it made a bit of difference?' Shoemaker's a fellow who'd tell you what he thought, and he said, 'I didn't think it made a bit of difference. The horse never lost not even a half inch of his momentum. I just raised my head up more or less.'"

It was always Jones' opinion that Gallant Man wouldn't have passed Iron Liege "if they had been going another time around."

Jones added: "Iron Liege was good right at that moment. When he was good, he was a better horse than people give him credit for being."

One final note on the '57 Derby: Lowe, whose dream had proven to be prophetic, won the fourth race two days later at Churchill Downs with a horse named Blenzie.

The name of the race?

The Dreamer Purse.

What First Wire?

In 1981, Sandy Hawley stood up aboard Partez, the Derby's third-place finisher.

Afterward, in the jockeys' room, Hawley provided this explanation: "There were a couple of horses—those two horses in front of me—and I had the dirt flying back in my face and when I got to the first wire, I kinda thought the race was over."

Two points here.

First of all, only one horse, the victorious Pleasant Colony, was ahead of Partez at the time that Hawley stood up in the irons. Woodchopper, who was third, would have needed magic hoofs to kick dirt in the face of a jockey who was *ahead* of him.

Here's what actually happened: Partez was running second and Woodchopper was coming up on his outside, about to overtake him, when Hawley raised up. Hawley stood up for four strides before he resumed riding.

Secondly, *what* first wire?

"At the sixteenth pole, right?" a reporter said to Hawley in an attempt to determine exactly at which point the jockey stood up.

"It was the first wire," said Hawley. "Is the first wire at the sixteenth pole?"

"No, there's just one wire there, I believe," the reporter replied.

"No, there's two wires," Hawley insisted. "There's two finish lines, right?"

No, Sandy, there's only one finish pole, only one wire.

"I must have stood up at the sixteenth pole," Hawley finally agreed.

Hawley had ridden in only one previous Derby, finishing third on Golden Act in 1979.

Hawley's mistake on Partez was more obvious than Shoemaker's stand-up bit on Gallant Man twenty-four years earlier. But where Shoemaker's error probably ruined Gallant Man's chance for victory, Hawley's mistake didn't affect the outcome of the Derby. Partez, who finished three lengths behind runner-up Woodchopper, might have run a closer third, but he was not going to win or finish second.

Keene Daingerfield, who was in the stewards' stand for the 1981 Derby, said that he was sure Hawley's mistake "cost his mount nothing, but I can't conceive of a

rider making that kind of error in a race of such importance."

Hampden Needed a Better Job

"Job Jessop is a real addition to the riding talent at the
New York tracks," stated *The Thoroughbred Record* magazine
in its April 27, 1946 issue. "So far, he has yet to make a
mistake in his handling of a mount in a race, and it would
appear that his leading the list in 1945 was no fluke."

For a rider who led American jockeys in total victories in
1945 and who was praised for not making mistakes, Jessop
was guilty of a boo-boo the very next month after the
magazine lauded him. He misjudged the finish line aboard
the Derby's third-place finisher, Hampden, who wasn't
going to get close to Assault, an eight-length winner. But if
it hadn't been for Jessop's mistake, Hampden (the 5.80–1
second choice) stood a good chance of finishing second
ahead of Spy Song, who gained runner-up honors by just a
head.

The Blood-Horse magazine reported: "The runner-up's
share might have gone to Hampden, but Jessop mistook
the gaudy sixteenth-pole for the finish and checked him
momentarily."

Reported *The Thoroughbred Record* magazine: "Spy Song
held on gamely but the camera had to decide whether he
had reached the wire before Hampden. The latter might
have been second had his rider, Jessop, not confused the
sixteenth pole with the finish line. Hampden lost ground
by that mistake although Jessop realized his error in a split
second and went to riding again for all he was worth."

Said *The Courier-Journal*: "Jessop might have brought
Hampden into second place but misjudged the finish line,
pulled his horse up momentarily before realizing his mistake, and then couldn't catch Spy Song when he got him
running again,"

Years later, Daingerfield said: "Assault was an easy winner, but Spy Song would never have kept second if Jessop hadn't eased his mount at the sixteenth pole. He realized his error and went back to riding, but too late."

In 1993, we placed a telephone call to the sixty-six-year-old Jessop and asked him about the '46 Derby.

Jessop disagreed with the idea that he might have finished second if he hadn't misjudged the finish line. "I wouldn't have been no closer than I was," he said. "I just raised up and dropped back down."

Told that the chart listed Hampden as finishing just a head behind second-place finisher Spy Song, Jessop replied, "That chart's wrong. I was beat a length. I wouldn't have been no closer."

Accounts of the '46 Derby finish showed, of course, that the chart was right: Spy Song edged Hampden by a head.

Explaining his mistake, Jessop said: "It was the first time I'd ever rode there. I had never seen the track. And the sixteenth pole at Churchill Downs is where the finish line would be on any other racetrack."

Were Hampden's people—owner William du Pont, Jr., and trainer Dick Handlen—upset afterward back at the barn? "Wel-l-l, not too much so," Jessop replied. "Of course, they were a little upset, but there wasn't much said about it. The owner was a little perturbed, but the trainer said, 'Oh, hell, it could happen to anybody. You wouldn't have been no closer anyway.'"

Jessop recalled that Hampden ran in the Preakness— "and the same horses just beat him easy."

Jessop didn't ride Hampden in the Preakness, though. Eddie Arcaro had the mount, and Hampden finished third again, this time 3¾ lengths behind the winner, Assault. In the Belmont, Hampden finished fourth under Arcaro, slightly more than five lengths behind the victorious Assault.

Could Jessop sympathize with Shoemaker following the

incident in the 1957 Derby? "Oh, very much so," Jessop
replied. "I'll say I could. Yeah, 'cause that's the height of
every jock's ambition—you know, to ride in the Derby and
then to win it. I always said I'd like to be national champion and win the Derby. I got to be national champion in
'45, but I never did get to win the Derby."

Did He or Didn't He?

Jean Cruguet knew what it felt like to cross the finish line
first in the Kentucky Derby. That's what he did aboard
Seattle Slew in 1977. He also knew what it felt like to stand
up as his mount passed the sixteenth pole in the Derby.
That's what he did aboard Play Fellow, the sixth-place finisher, in the 1983 Derby. Nothing was made of Cruguet's
action immediately after the race. The footnotes in the *Daily
Racing Form*'s chart originally didn't even mention the incident but later stated that Play Fellow "was hanging when
jockey Cruguet misjudged the finish line and rose for a
stride at the sixteenth marker, and finished out gamely."

In a 1993 interview, Cruguet disputed the *Form*'s comment that he misjudged the finish line. "They didn't come
to me [to find out] what I think about it," he said.

Cruguet said he knew where the finish line was. He did
acknowledge that he rose before the finish—"the race was
over for *me*"—but added that he didn't want to get fined
by the stewards for standing up too early, so he went back
to riding.

Two Finish Wires? Not So

Forty years after his 1935 Derby victory with Omaha,
Willie ("Smokey") Saunders looked back on the race and
said, "I think that's the longest stretch I ever looked down,
being in front and was sure hoping to get to the end of it
also. That was when they had the two finish wires, and I

very nearly pulled up, like Shoemaker did, and happened to look around and see Roman Soldier coming at me and I think I rode my horse clear into the backside to make sure that if we'd gone around again, I was gonna keep riding."

Did Saunders confuse the sixteenth pole with the finish? "No, they had an actual wire across there," he maintained. "They used to run some race, some stake, in the fall of the year, and they used that as the finish line, and they'd leave it up the whole time. That was the silliest thing in the world having two finish lines there. It's a funny thing, when you're riding a horse and you go under the wire, you just sense it and you automatically pull up. You assume that's the finish—I mean, which it is on every racetrack. But at Louisville they had two finish wires."

Saunders' memory might have been playing tricks on him about the two finish wires. After all, if Hawley imagined shortly after the '81 Derby that there were two finish wires, it's understandable how Saunders, 40 years later, would not have total—and accurate—recall on what had happened in 1935.

We once asked two veterans—Daingerfield and Louisville newspaperman Mike Barry—whether the Downs had two finish lines in 1935. Both said no.

"I think Smokey Saunders is dead wrong," Daingerfield declared. "He may, of course, have misjudged the finish line of the 1935 Derby—although the chart describes Omaha as an easy winner—but I am sure there were never two finish lines at Churchill Downs. For one thing, there would have been no conceivable reason for it. Smokey may be thinking about the mile-and-a-sixteenth finish line at Keeneland."

No, No, Sweet William

Bill Hartack misjudged the finish line during Derby Week in 1974 at the Downs. Yes, the same Bill Hartack who won the '57 Derby with Iron Liege after Shoemaker misjudged the finish line with Gallant Man. Hartack's blunder came in the National Turf Writers Association Purse, a race named in honor of a group with certain members who weren't exactly the best of friends with the outspoken jockey.

Not only that, but there was a clear message for Hartack in this race if only he had paid attention to the winner's name. Hartack, it seems, stood up just inside the sixteenth pole aboard Fun Co K., who was leading. The horse who was running second at that point proceeded to pass Fun Co K. and win the race by a head. All Hartack had to do was look back just before the sixteenth pole and ask the nearest horse to him his name. The reply would have told Hartack that what he was about to do was a no-no.

The horse's name was none other than No No Billy.

Trickery?

In the late 1940s, Tommy Barrow pulled up his horse at the Downs' sixteenth pole after he might have been tricked by a more experienced jockey. "I was in front, and the boy on the second horse, who was on the rail, stood up," Barrow once recalled. "I thought it was the finish and stood up, too. The boy on the other horse got back down quicker and beat me."

Oh, Baby

On opening day of the 1974 spring meeting, Jerry Friar misjudged the finish line aboard Sensitivo's Baby, a 39–1 long shot who came in first but was disqualified to third for causing interference in the stretch run.

Rudy's Oops

Rudy Turcotte might have cost his mount, Buddy Larosa, a victory at the Downs on November 9, 1976. Turcotte stood up momentarily after passing the sixteenth pole, then after realizing his mistake, dropped down and went to the whip. But he lost by a head to Khyber King.

(K)napping

On opening day of the 1965 fall meeting, Kenny Knapp stood up prematurely aboard Road Break in the first half of the daily double—a claiming race with a purse of $3,000. "It didn't make the daily double backers of Road Break very happy," wrote Dean Eagle, sports editor of *The Louisville Times*. "Whether he would have won is a moot point."

Eagle reported that afterward Knapp handled the incident well, showing "class" and "taking it like a man."

Said Knapp: "I goofed. The Churchill Downs stretch is so long, and it was my first race here in a long time. I'm glad it wasn't a more important race. At least, there is that consolation."

Knapp was right about two things: He did goof, and the Downs stretch is long. But he was misleading about another matter: Sure, he hadn't ridden at the Downs in a long time. Neither had any of the other jockeys on the card. It was the *first day* of the fall meeting. But he was anything but a stranger at the track. He had ridden at the Downs in the spring of 1965 and was the meeting's leading jockey with twenty-two victories in more than one hundred mounts.

How many rides does a guy need at a track to know his way around?

Too Tall

Tammy Trujillo stood tall aboard Optimum Mode on June 19, 1992. Too tall. See, the idea isn't to be standing tall. It's to be crouched down, riding the horse all the way to the finish line. Cliff Guilliams, chart caller for *Daily*

Racing Form, noted that Trujillo stood up prematurely in the irons "about ninety yards from the wire," then returned to riding in the last two strides. Tammy's mistake didn't influence the outcome of the race. Optimum Mode finished second, three lengths behind the winner.

For Cripe's Sake

In the fall of 1965, jockey J. Rosello stood up near the sixteenth pole and finished second aboard Sir Bop, a mistake that might have cost him the victory. Even so, those fans who wagered on Rosello's mount should have forgiven the jockey. As Bob Hurley of the *Daily Racing Form* put it, "Any jockey with a first name like Rosello's should be entitled to one mistake."

Rosello's first name?

Jesus.

Bracadale was officially listed as the fifth-place finisher in the 1924 Kentucky Derby, but he actually ran second or third. The placing judges mixed up his silks with those of Beau Butler. (Courtesy of Keeneland-Cook)

10

You Be the Judge
of the 1924 Derby Finish

IMAGINE YOURSELF IN THE PLACING JUDGES' STAND at the 1924 Kentucky Derby.

The field is thundering down the stretch in the fiftieth Derby at Churchill Downs, and your job—and that of two colleagues—is to name the official order of finish. Inside the sixteenth pole, four horses are battling it out in a furious finish, and it's all you can do to keep track of the horses. The crowd is roaring loudly, and the horses are reaching out mightily in the final desperate yards of this race. This is a great finish, one of the greatest you've ever seen, but you can't enjoy the excitement of the race so much because you have a job to do. You have to determine for this day, and for history, the order of finish in the Kentucky Derby.

Now the field of nineteen is coming toward the finish line, and the four on the front end remained in contention. They draw nearer and nearer to the line, and it's obvious that Black Gold is going to win. Everything else isn't so obvious to you. The first four horses are in a bunch—and, surprisingly enough, your view isn't the best at the track. Too bad you couldn't be up higher, up there where you could see with your own eyes which horse that is down there on the rail, the one virtually obscured by Black Gold.

Okay, the race is over, and you have just witnessed one of the closest four-horse finishes in Derby history. No Derby before, or since, has ever produced as close a battle among the first four finishers as the 1924 renewal.

What do you do?

Just be glad you weren't responsible for naming the order of finish in that '24 Derby, because it was no easy assignment.

The placing judges are like umpires. When things go smoothly, you hardly notice them. But when there's a controversy, they are thrust into the limelight.

The 1924 Derby produced quite a controversial finish.

Less than a length separated the four horses in the 1924 Derby. As they crossed under the wire, Black Gold clearly won by about a half-length.

With the horses close together and fighting it out to the wire, it appeared that Chilhowee might have been second. Or was it Bracadale who actually ran second? Or maybe even Altawood?

Why all the questions? Why not just check the film?

Well, it wasn't quite that simple back then.

Turn the clock back to the 1924 Derby and you'll find that the placing judges had to make their decision based solely on what they saw—or what they *thought* they saw—as the horses, so tightly bunched at the finish, whirled under the wire. There was no photo-finish camera to rely on in those days. No patrol film. No instant replays. Only the naked eye.

Times have changed. We take so many things for granted nowadays—the photographs, the videotape, the instant replays—but in 1924 the first time anybody would see a film of the Derby was the following day. And that was news in itself.

"Heretofore no motion picture concern has been able to reproduce pictures of the Derby in time to display them on the screen earlier than a week after the race," it was reported on Derby Eve. But in 1924, for the first time in Derby history, a film of the race could be seen the *very next day* in Louisville at the Alamo Theater.

If shortly after the Derby the judges could have seen a

sneak preview of that film. If only . . .

Those judges for the '24 Derby—J. S. ("Toney") Wallace, Noah H. McClelland, and E. B. Webb—named Chilhowee second and Beau Butler third.

Did somebody say Beau Butler finished third in the 1924 Derby?

Yes, the Downs placing judges did, and they were wrong.

It was Bracadale—and not Beau Butler—who finished third in that Derby. Some observers even insisted that Bracadale actually ran second. Bracadale, who was ridden by Earl Sande, and Mad Play ran in a Rancocas Stable entry that was the 3.40–1 second choice. Harry Sinclair and Sam Hildreth, the Rancocas owner and trainer, reportedly wagered $10,000 through the pari-mutuels to show on their entry, a bet on which they should have collected. The Rancocas people were said to have complained bitterly for weeks about this error, but their laments weren't going to change the decision made by the placing judges.

Beau Butler, owned by the Idle Hour Stock Farm Stable of Col. E. R. Bradley and ridden by Lawrence Lyke, was coupled with Baffling and Bob Tail. The Idle Hour threesome went off at 10.25–1. Baffling finished seventeenth, and Bob Tail brought up the rear in the field of nineteen. As for Beau Butler, according to different sources, he ran seventh or eighth—or maybe as far back as twelfth. But no way did he finish third.

Colonel Bradley was extremely popular in Kentucky, but there was no reason to think that he was being favored by the placing judges in this particular case. This error was so blatant that it couldn't have been anything but an honest mistake. Nobody in his right mind would try to pull something on the public in a such an obvious situation.

The silks of the four horses who actually finished within a length of each other shouldn't have presented a problem for the placing judges: old rose, white cross sashes and bars on sleeves, and black cap for Black Gold; brown, red bars on sleeves, and red cap for Chilhowee; white, green collar and cuffs for Bracadale; and blue, white bars on sleeves, and blue and white cap for Altawood.

But the problem was with the green-and-white silks of Bracadale's owner. They were too similar to those of Beau Butler's owner.

Keene Daingerfield, a veteran steward who as a youth saw his first Derby in 1924, years later shed some light on the controversy. "The error was generally explained as being the result of a mix-up in colors," Daingerfield explained. "Rancocas was white with green collar, cuffs, and cap. Col. E. R. Bradley had changed from white with green hoops to green and white vertical halves, with green hoops on the white half and white hoops on the green half. Hence, the colors appeared different on the backside and in the stretch. While this may have been confusing, when you analyze it, it doesn't furnish an adequate explanation. Anyhow, for many years after 1924, vertical halves were forbidden, and Colonel Bradley changed swiftly back to his old colors.

"I recall that Clyde Ponce, who finished far back on Mrs. Walter N. Jeffords' Diogenes, was visting the next day at Faraway Farm, which my Aunt Elizabeth Daingerfield was then managing for the Sam Riddles and the Jeffords, and commented on how surprised Lawrence Lyke had been when he saw his number on the board."

Besides the difficulty in distinguishing between the colors of the Rancocas and Idle Hour stables at the 1924 Derby was the fact that Bracadale was on the rail, with Chilhowee next to him and Black Gold on the outside. From their vantage point, which wasn't the best seat in the house to view such close finishes, the placing judges no doubt had difficulty in seeing Bracadale on the inside.

"The placing judges must not be criticized too harshly for their mistake and it was one that could hardly have happened if they were judging the finish from a higher elevation," declared the *Daily Racing Form*. "It has been

urged before that the judges should be at an elevation
where it would be possible to see over the top of the horses
and this mistake brings home that contention with pecu-
liar force. There are finishes so close that they have to be
sighted as one would sight a gun, but this sighting can
never identify the rail horse if he is covered up by the one
with which he is fighting for victory. This sighting will
discover the winner to the fraction of an inch, but it is of
no use unless it is possible at the same time to identify the
horses. Undoubtedly, Chilhowee was properly placed by
the sighting process, but it prevented the identification of
Bracadale and for that reason he was denied any share in
the prize while a horse that was not even fourth was moved
up into third position."

Nowadays, it would be virtually impossible for placing
judges to make such an error (particularly in a race of the
Derby's magnitude), but if they did, the media would roast
them. In 1924, the mistake didn't go undetected by journalists, but for the most part they weren't particularly
harsh in their observations.

Readers of Bruce Dudley's front-page story appearing
in *The Courier-Journal* had to flip to the jump page of his
prose to read that Beau Butler had turned in a "valorous"
effort following an unfavorable start, having "worked his
way from fifteen position at the quarter to eleventh at the
half; tenth at the three-quarter and tenth at the turn into
the stretch."

Dudley, who had a certain flair to his style and succeeded in a folksy sort of a way of imitating Grantland
Rice, knew very little about horse racing, but it was his
assignment to write the lead story in the newspaper. So
relying strictly on the Derby chart (which had to be adjusted to conform to the placing judges' error), he wrote
that "Beau Butler's dash's down the stretch was a heart
warming spectacle that can never be effaced."

In those days, *The Courier-Journal* would run Derby

accounts from out-of-town writers, and in that newspaper's sports section appeared two articles that conflicted
with Dudley's story and would have left readers scratching
their heads in wonderment about the Derby finish.

The *New York World*'s knowledgeable George Daley wrote:
"It is almost inconceivable that the judges could blunder
in the placing of the horses in such an important race.
Bracadale was completely overlooked for either second or
third place. The chart had to be corrected to meet the
official placing. It is not an accurate accounting of what
really happened. No doubt, the colors were mixed. Those
of the Rancocas Stable and E. R. Bradley are much alike at
some angles. . . . Bracadale, on the rail, was blanketed by
the other three so that his number could not be seen. Once
again it may be suggested that the judges should be more
elevated. The mistake was a hardship on the Rancocas
Stable and a hardship, too, on those who wagered on
the stable to be third. Honest mistakes are the hardest to
bear."

New York turf scribe G. F. T. Ryall, who later would
write for the *New Yorker* magazine under the name of Audax
Minor, observed after the '24 Derby that Sam Hildreth,
the trainer of Bracadale, believed that his colt "finished
second, a matter of inches in front of Chilhowee, and being on the inner rail, blanketed by Chilhowee and Black
Gold, with Sande crouched so low in the saddle, the judges
never saw him at all." Ryall wrote that this opinion was
substantiated by a number of "horsemen and keen judges"
who witnessed the race.

It was unfortunate that readers of *The New York Times*
didn't have access to a better reporting job than they received. *The Times* saw fit to print that Beau Butler "made a
great race of it to take down $3,000 of third money. Slow to
get away he never was in the hunt until the field was well
on the way home. Lyke rode a great finish and in that last
quarter mile he brought the colt up from tenth position to

land him a head in front of Altawood, losing the place to Chilhowee by only a nose."

Two days after the Derby, sports editor Robert E. Dundon of *The Louisville Herald* wrote: "Placing judges at a race track are like umpires in a ball game. They are constantly being called on to make close decisions, the sort that may be decided either way. For that reason this writer seldom disputes their finding and certainly always has been willing to accept it as final, the same as the ruling of a baseball arbiter."

Dundon, who wore glasses, went on to inform his readers that he believed he had "pretty good vision" and that he "called the Derby finish from the press stand as follows: Black Gold, first by a head; Bracadale, second, a nose; Chilhowee, third, half a length, then Altawood. When dealing with head and nose finishes from the angle, one is always possibly in error. There is also the possibility of mistaking colors. But it is seldom that you lose sight of the one particular horse whose every move you have watched from the flagfall, giving only a cursory glance at the others until the stretch battle is on. The way it seemed to us, Bracadale, on which Sande had the mount, set the pace for a mile and an eighth, when Chilhowee moved up alongside him. Bracadale was on the rail and the Gallaher colt outside him. Black Gold, which was in the clear, was outside this pair. Black Gold joined them about fifty yards from the wire, and it could be seen that he was striding more determinedly than his rivals. He also had more open space to run in, the others being 'packed' against the rail. . . .

"In writing his account of the Derby the writer naturally deferred to the consensus of opinion, which was that we had made an error and that the horse on the rail which we thought was Bracadale was, in fact, Beau Butler. We certainly are willing to admit that Chilhowee could have been second as easily as third, the place we thought he took."

Dundon concluded his story with this thought: "If there really was an error in the placing of the horses no great harm was done. The reason is that if Bracadale has been awarded second money there would have been good cause to disqualify him for the way that Sande interfered with some of the starters at the break. This would have left it practically the same way."

In *The Louisville Times*, Vernon ("Gimme a Match") Sanders wrote: "I saw the race myself from the press stand, and, while there was a rush of several horses for the goal right at the end, I will say that I never saw Beau Butler in the first division. He may have been there, though, as the finish was so close and the excitement so great that I am not going to set myself up against such competent racing officials as 'Toney' Wallace, Noah McClelland, and E. B. Webb, whose reputation for accuracy and ability have placed them in the front rank of racing officials in the country. If these three say that Beau Butler was third, this judgment rules and holds.

"In any event, in racing there seldom is such a thing as 'going behind the returns.' The placing judges said the finish was Black Gold, Chilhowee, and Beau Butler. The Jockey Club divided the public's money between these three in their respective positions, and it behooves all good sportsmen to abide by the decision of the placing judges."

Sanders observed that if the placing judges erred, "it was an honest mistake," adding that it was "an error of mistaken identity in the horse."

Three days after the Derby, *The Courier-Journal* itself got around to printing a story about the disputed finish. Bruce Dudley led off his story with this quote from Wallace, the dean of the three placing judges and also the Downs racing secretary: "The infallibility of man doesn't exist."

Dudley went on to quote Wallace as saying: "If I called the race correctly, I care not what may be the criticism. But if an error was made, I am woefully sorry. It is my firmest belief that the horses came in precisely as I called them. I could see 50 yards out that the finish was going to be close, and we were all bent to the task of tagging the horses as they nosed the line. Mr. McClelland called the horses as I called them, and so did Mr. Webb. If we are wrong, it is a question of eyesight."

Two days after the Derby, *The Louisville Times* had run a front-page story that made the placing judges look like they all needed to make immediate appointments with an eye doctor. A photograph of the finish showed an unidentified horse whose saddlecloth number was obscured by Black Gold. The photograph revealed that the horse, who was on the rail, was wearing blinkers and had a distinct blaze on his head. Chilhowee and Altawood, officially listed as the second- and fourth-place finishers, respectively, didn't wear blinkers. Bracadale wore blinkers and had just such a blaze. Beau Butler, on whom the Downs paid off at a $4.70 show mutuel, had the blinkers—but not the blaze.

A newspaper photograph, however, wasn't convincing proof, as far as placing judge Wallace was concerned. "Pictures taken at an angle form an optical illusion, an indisputable fact, and as all pictures of the Derby that I have seen were taken at an angle, they are of no value as evidence of the position of any horse at the finish," Wallace was quoted as saying.

Wallace was right about photographs. Depending on the angle they're taken, they can be misleading when it comes to close finishes. But the most misleading thing about the 1924 Derby weren't any of the photographs. The most misleading thing about that Derby was the decision by the placing judges that Beau Butler finished third. It never happened.

At the time, Wallace was quoted as saying: "Sorrowfully and with depressing regret will I admit that I called the finish wrong when proof can be shown of an error, but no statement or no picture has been carried to me yet that brought an approach to conviction with it. Enthused turf patrons, like enthused baseball fans, I respectfully submit, often think that they are the victims of erroneous decisions when they are not."

Wallace was told that Hildreth, the trainer of Bracadale, returned to New York after the Derby and "broadcast the information that he had been given a questionable decision in the Derby." To which Wallace replied: "I am sorry that Sam thinks so, but he knows me well enough to be assured that I never could wittingly do him or any other trainer or owner on the turf an injustice. It is only natural that he, as well as all Bracadale enthusiasts, should give that horse the benefit of any doubt."

Asked if the elevation of the judges' stand would assist him and his colleagues, Wallace said, "The very fact that spectators who are in the grandstand above us believe that they have seen the Derby finish more correctly than we who are right at the wire is an influence for a trial of the elevation of our pergola."

It's unfortunate that the Louisville press didn't bother to interview the Bradley people. It would have made for good reading back in 1924.

"We laughed when they put our horse's number up," said Olin Gentry, a longtime Bradley employee, said in an interview nearly fifty years later. "Beau Butler didn't finish third. Bracadale was third. Beau Butler was seventh or eighth."

In those days, before the advent of the starting gate, horses were sent on their way from the web barrier, which consisted of a net webbing, or tape, spread across the track. At the start, this tape was sent up and away—and the horses were off and running. Sometimes this method presented problems, as Gentry recalled regarding Beau Butler's start in the '24 Derby. "The tape got wrapped around the old jock's neck," Gentry said, "and he was practically left at the post, Beau Butler was. He came from way the hell back. He ran a big race to even be in the middle of the field [at the finish]."

J. Howard Rouse, another Kentucky horseman, saw it the same way, except that he said Beau Butler finished even farther back—in twelfth place. "Beau Butler got caught up in the web barrier at the start," Rouse said years later. "He was dragging part of the starting tape along behind him the first time past the stands. It was tangled in his bit, but then he either stepped on it or some other horse stepped on it because he got free of it. I was watching him the whole time because I thought he'd be a good bet in his next race. I know he finished 12th because I counted back to him."

It turned out that Beau Butler, despite his bad trip in the Derby, wouldn't have been a good bet in his next race. In the 1¼-mile Grainger Memorial Handicap a week after the Derby at the Downs, he finished fifth. He wouldn't have been a good bet the rest of his starts that year as well. He lost all five.

As for Bracadale, he came back from his strong effort in the Derby to win the Wither Stakes thirteen days later.

Jack L. Dempsey, the sharp-eyed chart caller for *Daily Racing Form*, called Bracadale—not Beau Butler—third at the finish of the Kentucky Derby. In order to conform to the official order of finish as seen through the eyes of the placing judges, the chart then had to be changed and Beau Butler was listed as the third-place horse, slightly more than a half-length behind Black Gold. At the stretch call, Beau Butler was in tenth place, a full 13¼ lengths off the lead. When the leader hit the top of the stretch in the 1961 Kentucky Derby, Carry Back was slightly more than thirteen lengths off the pace, but this great runner had what it took to make up that deficit and go on to win the roses by three-quarters of a length.

Beau Butler had won the Pimlico Futurity as a two-year-old, which proved to be the only stakes victory of his career. No candidate for racing's Hall of Fame, Beau Butler could never be confused with Carry Back.

The last quarter of a mile in the 1924 Derby was timed in twenty-six seconds. As far back as Beau Butler was turning for home, he would have needed to run the final quarter in faster than twenty-four seconds to finish as close to the front as the placing judges said he did. He would have needed the wings of Secretariat to make up that much ground. Dempsey's comments in the footnotes said: "Beau Butler closed a great gap and ran an excellent race." What else could Dempsey say? That Beau Butler was caught up in the tape at the start, was no factor, but was erroneously placed third by the judges?

Certain photographs of the Derby showed four horses within a length or so of each other nearing the finish. Depending on the angle of the photograph, not all four showed up clearly, except for Black Gold, the leader, and Altawood, on the outside. Bracadale's blazed face can barely be noticed in one photograph taken from the side, and Chilhowee, between Black Gold and Bracadale, was virtually obscured in another shot. The *Daily Racing Form* chart listed Black Gold as winning by a half-length over Chilhowee, with Beau Butler a nose back in third, Altawood a head back in fourth, and Bracadale another head back in fifth. With no photo-finish camera available, it's anybody's guess as to the exact order among the second-, third-, and fourth-place finishers. But one thing is crystal clear: There were four horses, not five, bunched together at the wire. Forget what the chart says. It had to be adjusted due to the placing judges' error. Although the chart has five horses within a length of each other at the finish, the newspaper and magazine photographs told the truth: There were only four. How can history resolve this problem? Contrary to what Bruce Dudley wrote in 1924 that

Beau Butler's charge down the stretch could never be effaced, the argument here is that it should be erased for one very good reason: It never happened.

One interesting point about *The Thoroughbred Record* magazine's cover shot of the 1924 Derby finish. If the placing judges had anything like the view of the finish that the photographer did, it's no wonder that they messed up. Bracadale is all but obscured, only a portion of his blazed face showing.

If the placing judges erred, then what was the actual finish of the 1924 Derby? We'll never know the answer to that question, but the idea here is that, judging from the finish photographs appearing in the Louisville newspapers and *The Thoroughbred Record*, it was Black Gold, first; Bracadale, second; Chilhowee, third; and Altawood, fourth.

The Beau Butler-Bracadale mixup has been a part of Derby lore for years, but almost completely overlooked was the contention of Lawrence ("Pud") McDermott, the jockey aboard Altawood, that his mount finished second, not fourth, in that race.

Fifty years after the '24 Derby, McDermott recalled the race almost as if it had happened just the day before. "There were 19 starters in the race to start off with," McDermott told this writer in a telephone interview, "and at the three-eighths pole I was last. I didn't have a horse beat. I couldn't get through, so I went around 18 horses.

"When they headed for home, when they turned down in the stretch, Earl Sande [aboard Bracadale] and Albert Johnson [riding Chilhowee] were running head and head. And Black Gold run by them about the eighth pole, and I was running by them, about, well, I'd say about 70 yards from the wire.

"Now I'm sitting here, I got a picture in my hand of the finish. It was taken from the infield. And I would say at this point Black Gold is just about three-quarters of a length from the finish line. Now Earl Sande's down on the rail. I'm on the outside of Albert Johnson, and the picture shows me about a head in front of him at that point. And I had come from about 11th or 12th at the head of the stretch. I was moving by all three of them [Black Gold, Chilhowee, and Bracadale] on the outside. I was in front a jump past the wire. That's how fast I was runnin'."

There was no question in McDermott's mind that the placing judges had made a mistake. "I'll go to my grave saying that I wind [sic] up second in the race," he said.

One story had it that Sande thought he came in second aboard Bracadale, but McDermott said: "Sande swore he finished third in the race."

The jockeys didn't make an issue of the controversy afterward, McDermott said. "Back in those days, why, there was two things that riders never done. They never claimed foul on another rider in the race, regardless of what the interference was, and they accepted the stewards' and the placing judges' decision. They never put up any beef about it. However they placed them or whatever the stewards done, why, they accepted it."

According to the *Form*'s chart, Altawood trailed by some 5½ lengths at the stretch call and came on to lose by slightly more than a half-length. He was, in the words of one story, "one of the sensations of the running. He was one of the unfortunates through the early stages and closed an immense gap to finish fourth. At the end he was racing better than the three that finished in front of him, and many good judges expressed the opinion that he would have been the winner in another sixteenth."

Another account said: "Altawood probably ran the best race of all. He was a trailer down the back stretch but when he made his move he fairly ran over horses."

Altawood certainly was a fine racehorse, winning the Blue Grass Stakes, Bowie Handicap, and Latonia Cup Handicap in 1924 and the Jockey Club Gold Cup and

Pimlico Cup Handicap in 1925. The Latonia Cup and Pimlico Cup were 2¼-mile marathons, and in the former he equaled the track record of 3:49.

McDermott was asked if there was anything said in the jockeys' room after the '24 Derby. "No, there was no comments made in the jocks' room," he said. "Riders kept things pretty well to themselves regardless of what they thought."

One final note to this controversy. Bradley, the owner of Beau Butler, was a famous gambler who liked to make side bets. According to one story, Bradley had made a $5,000 horse-against-horse Derby wager with Harry Sinclair, the Rancocas Stable owner. The winner of the bet would be the owner of whichever horse—Beau Butler or Bracadale—finished ahead of the other. One story is that Bradley collected on the bet.

But another account declared that Sinclair sent Bradley a check for $5,000 after the Derby. So this story goes, Bradley reportedly tore the signature off the check and mailed it back to Sinclair, saying that Bracadale had beaten Beau Butler.

Mrs. Elizabeth Arden Graham at Hialeah Park in 1942. (Courtesy Keeneland-Cook)

11

Mrs. Lipstick Won the 1947 Derby with the Cosmetic Kid

Wanted: Trainer (and baby sitter) for a major horse racing stable.

Prerequisites: Patience (with the owner).

Experience: Would help if applicant has background in applying Elizabeth Arden creams (on horses).

Warning: Don't be alarmed if owner calls at all hours to check on horses climbing trees (sweet dreams).

Job security: You're kidding.

Contact: Mrs. Lipstick (a.k.a. Mrs. Mudpack).

Elizabeth Arden Graham, the cosmetics queen, never took out such an advertisement. None was needed. Trainers who went to work for her Maine Chance Farm had advance warning of her idiosyncrasies and didn't expect to stay on the job forever.

A job with her sometimes didn't last much longer than an application of her eight-hour cream. Trainers came and went from Maine Chance as if they were whirling through a revolving door. One minute a trainer had his foot in the barn, the next minute he was on the outside looking in. It became a standard game around the racetrack to attempt to name all of the persons who had ever worked for Mrs. Graham.

As master of ceremonies at the Kentucky Thoroughbred Breeders Association's annual Kentucky Derby trainers' dinner in 1954, Churchill Downs president Bill Corum said, "I checked with the Associated Press and other news sources before dinner and found that the next speaker, Mr. Eddie Neloy, still is trainer for Maine Chance."

Neloy promptly updated Corum. "I have even later news," Neloy told the audience. "I have just talked with New York. As of 9:17 P.M., I *still* am the trainer!"

Soon after joining Maine Chance, Neloy was asked how long he had been with the stable. "Eight days and a half," he replied.

Less than a month after the 1954 Derby, Neloy had another job. "E. A. ('Eddie') Neloy reversed the usual pattern of Maine Chance trainers by resigning before he was fired," reported *The Blood-Horse*. The magazine noted that his Maine Chance tenure lasted all of about six weeks. Black Metal, owned by Maine Chance, had finished thirteenth in the Derby that year, but stablemate Fascinator had won the Kentucky Oaks on Derby Eve.

Mrs. Graham's horse operation was a colorful one, in more ways than one. In the book, *Miss Elizabeth Arden*, it was pointed out that her Belmont barn "was painted in her racing colors, cherry-pink, white, and blue. Plants were hung over the stalls, and soothing music was piped in. Blue and pink cashmere blankets protected her little darlings from draughts, and the jockeys' silks, custom-made of the finest taffeta available, were sent to the best dry cleaner in the city, a man who ordinarily handled only Paris originals and charged prices very nearly as exorbitant as the original cost of the garments."

An anonymous trainer was quoted in the book as saying: "When I was a kid, my mother used to say, 'Only horses sweat. People perspire.'" But that wasn't true in the Maine Chance stable, the trainer said. "Over there, the horses perspire. It's the trainers who sweat."

The book also referred to the time Mrs. Graham called the Mayo Clinic when one of her horses became sick. A specialist, indignant, refused to diagnose for a horse.

"What would you do if he were a baby?" she demanded.

"I wouldn't enter him in the Santa Anita Handicap," the doctor replied, hanging up.

Trainers wished they could hang up on Mrs. Graham on occasion.

Veteran horsemen still chuckle when recalling the time that Mrs. Graham once called trainer Monte Parke in the middle of the night at a Belmont Park cottage and told him that she had just had a dream that a filly of hers was up in a tree outside the barn.

"Would you please go out and check on her?" Mrs. Graham supposedly asked the trainer.

Just to get her off the phone, the trainer replied, "Mrs. Graham, yeah, I'll go out there and look and see if she's out there, sure."

Click.

A short time later, Parke called up Mrs. Graham.

"Did you check on that filly?"

"You know, Mrs. Graham, I climbed all the way up in that tree," said Parke, who had never left the bedroom. "And I went in the stall, and if she was up there, she got back in that stall all right. Everything's fine."

Another version of that story had Mrs. Graham calling Parke and saying, "I had a dream that one of my babies was out underneath the apple tree eating green apples. You know he'll get the colic. Will you go see?"

"Well, we've got two night watchmen."

"Well, you just go out there under that old apple tree."

She telephoned back and was assured by Parke not to worry. "Yeah, I went out there," he told her. "There's nothing out there. All the horses are in the stalls."

Training for Mrs. Graham required a horseman to add certain things to his stable repertoire that otherwise might be found in a beauty salon. She would send her Arden Skin Lotion and Elizabeth Arden Eight Hour Cream to the barn by the cases to be used on her horses. "Rub this on the horses and it'll get rid of skin disease," she told her trainers.

Her products, all expensive, would cover blemishes and were used on bites and pimples. Furthermore, Mrs. Graham seemed to think the sweet-smelling creams and skin lotions would help horses relax.

"That eight-hour cream was good for sores, there's no question about it," recalled Ivan Parke, who trained Maine Chance horses for more than a year. "It was good for cracked heels. It would heal. I used it on cracked heels—not only when I was with her but even afterwards. She give me the idea of it."

But some trainers didn't particularly like the idea of horses being massaged and conditioned with such products. Other trainers, trying to keep peace with Mrs. Graham, would obediently apply the stuff. One way around the problem was to keep her creams and lotions on display in front of the horses' stalls while she was around. Then when she'd leave the barn, the stablehands would pack all her products away in a tack room. That's not all some of these lads would do behind her back. They'd also call her Mrs. Mudpack.

Certain grooms—trainers, too, for that matter—would carry her creams and lotions home. Some grooms were even known to take her products away and sell them at discounted prices.

A story in *The Saturday Evening Post* told of her relationship with grooms. "With her grooms Miss Arden finds herself up against the few persistent cases of human insubordination in her lifetime. She simply cannot make these happy-go-lucky, irresponsible characters do what she wants them to. If she annoys them too much, they throw down their rub rags and quit."

Mrs. Graham once fired her best exercise boy because she could not stand the sight of his hair, which was described as "remarkably bushy and profuse."

All Mrs. Graham wanted around the stable was one thing—her way. She even wanted perfume sprayed in the stalls. A stablehand who once worked for her said, "I think she believes horses run better after their stables have been done over by some wacky interior decorator."

One of her trainers wasn't inclined to get up extra early in the morning. Instead, he'd arrive at the barn at 8 A.M., showered and shaved. One morning, the trainer showed up at the barn and walked over to Mrs. Graham, who had been there since 7 A.M. "I think this job is too much for you," Mrs. Graham informed him. "Your contract has eight more months to run. I'll pay it, but you're fired."

The steady stream of trainers coming and going sometimes led to confusion. During one fall in Kentucky, Mrs. Graham had some broodmares in her consignment at a sale. She was sitting on a bench outside a barn, and trainer Mack Miller spoke to her casually and politely.

"Come here, young man," she said. "I want to see you."

"Yes, ma'am," said Miller. "What can I do?"

"You cost me some money," said Mrs. Graham.

"Mrs. Graham, what do you mean?"

"Well, my general manager hired you to train my horses, and I signed the contract. But when you walked into my shed the next day, you had Texas boots, you were much shorter, and you had a cowboy hat on."

"Well, Mrs. Graham, you obviously made a mistake."

It turned out that Mack Miller's name had been confused with that of the trainer who was mistakenly hired—Freeman McMillan.

"I had to pay him off," Mrs. Graham told Miller. "He was a perfectly nice man, but I didn't want *him*."

Recalling the incident, Miller said, "She laughed about it for several years after that. She would see me and say, 'Hello, Tex. How are you?'"

Four of Mrs. Graham's horses once were sent to Miller at

Keeneland. That's not all that was sent. "She had four cases of pure olive oil in the shipment," said Miller.

Miller said a cup of olive oil was given to the horses in their feed every afternoon. "And do you know what? They were the best-looking horses I ever saw," said Miller. "I never saw such coats in my life. I know the olive oil did it. Most people couldn't afford it, but she did."

Money was no obstacle to Mrs. Graham. "Most of the people did, in fact, get contracts and most of them didn't last long, but they were always paid off," said Miller. "She was really a delightful lady—smart, obviously a good businesswoman. But the horse business just defeated her. She was not practical in any respect of this business. She was very fussy about her horses. She loved animals. They were considered her children and her pets. She wanted horses treated precisely like humans. She had quite a lot of luck as it was, but if she had turned it over to some man and said, 'Look, you run it,' and left him alone, I'll tell you she would have broken up this game."

The long line of trainers who worked for Mrs. Graham included Louis Feustel and Max Hirsch, Clarence Buxton and Eddie Holton, Silent Tom Smith and Jimmy Smith, Eddie Neloy and George Poole, Monte Parke and Ivan Parke. The list goes on and on. Some of her trainers would quit or be fired, only to return for a second or even a third tour of duty later on.

One trainer, Jack Skirvin, went to work for Mrs. Graham in February of 1949. Two months later, a newspaper ran a headline stating: "It Happened." What in the name of Helena Rubinstein happened? He had resigned, of course.

George Poole trained for Mrs. Graham in 1963. "I trained for her from February through August," Poole said. "I think that was a long tenure—one of the longer uninterrupted ones."

Poole enjoyed that training stint, for the most part. "I left her on good terms," he said. "I got along good with her. We had our differences, but she more than made up for them. She went first rate. She was all right. I have very fond memories of her."

Poole recalled how Mrs. Graham would baby her horses. "They talk about horseflesh being dumb. She was always giving them sugar and any delicacy she thought they'd possibly eat. They knew her when she came down the shed. They'd go to hollering just like they do when you get ready to put the feed tubs in. I'll say one thing about her: She really loved animals. That was no put-on. She had a tremendous soft spot in her heart for animals. She had an old mutt that she picked up somewhere that lived like a queen over there in her apartment."

Poole once vanned Gun Bow a short distance from Delaware Park to Garden State Park the day of a race. Such trips are commonplace, but Mrs. Graham thought it was, oh, so demanding to transport Gun Bow on a van early in the morning. "This poor horse was just *way* down in Delaware," she told Poole.

"Well, Mrs. Graham, it's only down the pike a piece."

"You and those damned Kentuckians. That pike a piece, that's liable to mean anything."

Gun Bow won by ten lengths, and afterward everything was fine with Mrs. Graham.

Mrs. Graham once was showing Poole, the groom, and the foreman how to apply some of her cream to a horse.

Poole, holding the horse, put some of the cream on his own face. He was mocking Mrs. Graham, but she thought he was serious. She turned and said, "Oh, I'm *certainly* glad I have a trainer that realizes I put out good products."

"I get a little blemish now and again," Poole told her, "and I just think this is great."

"*At least* you have some sense," replied Mrs. Graham.

Mrs. Graham, who associated with some of the most famous people in the world, was an attractive, petite woman with immense vitality. A believer in improving beauty and the breed, she likened her two interests by saying, "I judge a woman and a horse by the same standards—legs, head, and backside." She also said, "Treat a horse like a woman and a woman like a horse and they'll both win for you."

On a 1953 owner's license application, she listed her eyes as blue, her hair as blonde, her weight as 110 pounds, and her height at 5 feet, 2 inches. Her age? *21+*.

Mrs. Graham's exact age remained a mystery. At the time of her death, she was reported to be 81, 82, or 84. She always looked younger than her age. As *The New York Times* wrote in her obituary, she was "undeniably ageless, a circumstance that she accentuated by concealing her birth date. Whatever it may have been, Mrs. Graham, in her 60s and 70s, looked 20 years younger, even on close inspection of her face. Moreover, her hair never grayed publicly, but remained mostly a beige-blond."

She was called a "little dictator," and indeed she did expect her orders to be carried out by her employees. She was moody and erratic, she was a perfectionist, and she was iron-willed.

But she was charitable, too, donating her time and money to various causes.

She had a sincere affection for her horses. "I just love horses and can't bear to see them treated badly," said Mrs. Graham, who was twice-married and twice-divorced.

She'd address her horses in baby talk, calling them "babies" and "darlings" and "dears." She was known to kiss them, and they would appear on the track with lipstick on their noses. Her instructions to a jockey sometimes would include the order: "Don't hit my baby!"

It was often reported that Mrs. Graham wouldn't permit a jockey to use a whip on her horses. "This may have been true early in her career on the turf, and she never liked to see one of her fillies whipped excessively," reported the *Daily Racing Form*. "But after Jet Action lost the Sysonby of 1955 [by a head] to High Gun, she complained bitterly that

Hedley Woodhouse had not whipped the colt energetically enough. Actually, he had been whacked every stride of the final furlong."

The *Form* added: ". . . it is not true, as often published, that she never bet on her horses, but her wagers were extremely modest. Also, she was an intense rooter, though a quiet one, pounding the edge of her box—or a friend's arm—with her tiny fist as her horses came through the stretch."

Mrs. Graham raced champions Star Pilot, Beaugay, Rose Jet, Myrtle Charm, and Jewel's Reward. She bred Gun Bow, an earner of $798,722, and owned Lord Boswell, the 1945 Experimental Free Handicap highweight.

Lord Boswell ran with Maine Chance stablemates Knockdown and Perfect Bahram in the 1946 Derby. The three-horse entry was favored.

Derby Week in 1946 was not a happy time for Mrs. Graham. Two days before the Derby she lost twenty-three horses (all but one were two-year-olds) in a devastating fire at Arlington Park. Shocked by the loss, Mrs. Graham said the blaze was "just too terrible to talk about." She preferred to discuss the Derby, saying, "Yes, I would like to see Lord Boswell and Knockdown finish one-two in the Derby, but if Perfect Bahram does the big job, that would please me immensely. I believe each of our horses has a good chance. Some say I favor Lord Boswell, but that isn't true. Others have kidded me about not liking Knockdown, but I love that horse just as much as I love Lord Boswell, Perfect Bahram, and all my horses."

To her dismay, the Maine Chance entry failed in the Derby.

But another Maine Chance horse won on the Derby Day card. Jet Pilot would have been at Arlington Park in the fire that killed the Maine Chance horses, but instead he and another two-year-old had been sent to Churchill Downs with the stable's Derby threesome. Jet Pilot won his career debut by nine lengths on Derby Day in 1946, prompting some observers to predict, "There's your Derby winner next year."

Mrs. Graham had purchased Jet Pilot for $41,000 at a Keeneland yearling sale. He went on to earn $198,740 and to be called the Cosmetics Kid.

Jet Pilot won his first four races, each at a different track—Churchill Downs, Pimlico, Belmont, and Aqueduct. He then lost seven in a row before capturing the $1\frac{1}{16}$-mile Pimlico Futurity, his longest race before the Derby. As a three-year-old, Jet Pilot received only a pair of Derby preps. He finished sixth in the San Felipe and won the Jamaica Handicap.

Going into the Derby, Jet Pilot was considered by many to be strictly a sprinter. But he was in the hands of veteran Tom Smith. "Tom was, you might say, the dean of trainers," recalled Louisvillian Bill Lyons, who was Jet Pilot's exercise boy before the Derby. "He was really an excellent man with a horse. A speed horse he could make him go on. And he *did* make this horse go on."

Smith had lost his license in 1945 on a charge that a drug had been administered to a Maine Chance horse. Mrs. Graham stood by Smith, hiring his defense attorney. Smith lost his case, but Mrs. Graham used his son, Jimmy, as trainer until the suspension was over. She then brought the elder Smith back to train for Maine Chance.

Despite his supposed lack of staying power, Jet Pilot was the Derby's second choice at 5–1. The longest shot in the race was Jett-Jett, owned by William Peavey. Jett-Jett unseated his jockey at the post and ran off a quarter of a mile before being brought back to the gate. He should have been sent back to his barn instead. He finished dead last. "Certainly Mr. Peavey had every right to run his horse, having paid $1,050 for that privilege and no doubt he had some reason for doing so," wrote the noted Joe Palmer. "I merely wonder what it was."

Eddie Arcaro had the mount on the favored Phalanx, who proved to be the champion three-year-old colt of 1947. But he didn't win the Derby because of a combination of Tom Smith's training and Eric Guerin's brilliant ride aboard Jet Pilot, along with a not-so-brilliant ride by Arcaro.

"I knew the race was won when he got in front at the start," said Mrs. Graham, who didn't bet the first dime on Jet Pilot. "There's something about Tom Smith that gives you confidence. Last year, I nearly died during the race, but I just wasn't the least bit nervous today. I'm so very happy. We're going to celebrate with champagne tonight."

As she left the presentation stand, she added, "I think my jinx is over." She was referring not only to the fire of 1946 but to Smith's earlier suspension.

As fate would have it, the loss by a Maine Chance Farm horse in the 1946 Preakness had a bearing on the victory by Jet Pilot in the 1947 Derby. In the Preakness Arcaro didn't do the Maine Chance's Lord Boswell, ridden by Doug Dodson, any favors. Arcaro, aboard Hampden, either shut off Lord Boswell or held him in a switch. Once free, Lord Boswell wound up finishing a fast-closing second to Assault. "I had to check for an instant, and I was beaten a neck," Dodson once recalled. "Was I ever hot!"

Dodson, remembering what Arcaro had done to him, planned for the entire next year to get even. He got his revenge in the '47 Derby aboard Faultless. While Dodson and Arcaro were all too interested in what the other guy was doing, Guerin set a leisurely pace aboard Jet Pilot, who had just enough in reserve to win. Guerin held Jet Pilot together through the long homestretch to edge Phalanx by a head. Faultless was another head back in third.

"All Dodson kept doing was turning around looking for me," said Arcaro. "He was zeroing in on me, and Guerin was a good enough rider that he didn't move until he had to, and by that time it was too late for me. I had to steer wide around him [Dodson] at the head of the stretch. It cost me a lot of ground. I thought Phalanx was so much the best."

Syl Veitch, the trainer of Phalanx, recalled that Arcaro and Dodson "were watching one another, and I think that the other horse [Jet Pilot] just stole away on them. They thought he'd come back to them, and he didn't come back. A speed horse like that, you let them run in hand, they're liable to run four miles for you. You never know. A given day is the day they'll run the race of their life."

Jet Pilot ran the race of his life in the Derby. And he never won again, finishing out of the money in the Preakness and Withers before he was retired.

At the time of their greatest triumph, the 1947 Derby, it would seem that the relationship between Smith and Mrs. Graham would have been at its best. It wasn't.

Bill Lyons, the exercise rider for Jet Pilot, recalled that after the Derby Mrs. Graham and some of her guests went to the barn to look at the winner . . . and look at him . . . and look at him. "After the horse cooled out and was put in the stall, Mrs. Graham wanted him brought out time after time just for her friends to look at him in the shed," Lyons said. "Tom got in his car and left. He got so disgusted. He wanted his horse to rest and get over the race. Of course, these people were exuberant. They had just had a Derby winner—and I can understand that—but it didn't show much respect for that horse."

Why would horsemen put up with Mrs. Graham? "She'd offered such fabulous salaries to trainers, why, they'd have to accept it," Lyons said. "You'd be a fool to turn it down, hoping to hit on that magic formula that you could get along with her and wind up keeping the job over a month."

"Very few of them did," Lyons added, chuckling.

Lyons remembered that for his part as Jet Pilot's exercise rider Mrs. Graham "sent me a rather gracious gratuity for this horse winning the Derby."

Mrs. Graham indeed ran a Grade-A operation. Trouble

was, the *A* all too often stood for argument. Tom Smith himself resigned later in 1947. He returned to Maine Chance in 1949 but left again the following year, reportedly parting on friendly terms. In 1953, he again took a position as Maine Chance trainer, but once more the job didn't last long.

Shortly after the Derby, John H. Clark wrote in *The Thoroughbred Record* magazine: "Tom Smith was on the verge of resigning as trainer for Maine Chance Stable a week or so before the Derby—and he may quit yet!"

In a 1980 article in the same magazine, Clark wrote that Mrs. Graham "remains today as one of my most 'unforgettable' persons. I served as consultant to her on matters concerning the Thoroughbred for four years preceding her death in 1966. Never have I had a client more appreciative of my feelings—or my work.

"This was not so with jockeys, trainers, and farm managers. She fired them upon the slightest whim. One trainer was hired one morning and sacked four hours later! Trainer Monte Parke was told to stop chewing tobacco or be dismissed."

Another item written by Clark referred to Mrs. Graham's feeling that she "needed a secret informer to keep her apprised of any irregularities or contraventions of her orders in her racing stable. She had a dandy in a young man whose nickname was Chico. Each succeeding Maine Chance trainer had to agree as a condition of employment to retain Chico as a groom. Chico was remunerated quite handsomely on the side for these services.

"Once Miss Arden transferred Chico to her Maine Chance Farm at Lexington for the same purposes. Upon his arrival, the young Latin announced to the farm manager, Jim Lockwood, 'I take care of only three horses, just like in the racing stable,' so Jim acceded to his wishes. When the other farm workers complained, Jim asked and got their forbearance. Jim *did* know how to handle Miss Arden.

"When asked by her how things were going upon her arrival a few days later, Jim sheepishly noted there was a 'labor problem . . . Chico has convinced the other grooms they shouldn't have to care for nine horses, only three.' That did it. Miss Arden immediately sent Chico back to her stable in New York."

In another article, Clark wrote of the time that Mrs. Graham arrived at her barn at Belmont Park and found two grooms sitting down on the job.

"Both of you are fired," she informed them.

"Oh, no, Miss Arden, you can't fire me," one of them told her. "I'm just visiting. I work for Max Hirsch."

Mrs. Graham wasn't at a loss for words. "Well, I'll have Mr. Hirsch fire you—you should be working. I'll tell him."

She told Hirsch, who proceeded to fire the groom.

Mrs. Graham, who bought her first Thoroughbred in the early 1930s, was America's leading money-winning owner in 1945 with $589,170. She was so devoted to her horses that she couldn't stand to part with them. Sometimes when she'd sell her yearlings at auctions, she'd wind up doing what many women do at sales—she'd change her mind and buy the horses back.

A case in point was Jewel's Reward. Put in a 1956 Saratoga sale, he didn't awe prospective buyers and Mrs. Graham ended up buying the yearling back herself for $3,500. Veteran horsemen thought that Mrs. Graham had an overinflated opinion of the colt's value, but she said, "I knew he was a better horse than that."

She named the colt Jewel's Reward, believing he'd be a reward for her faith and confidence in his sire, Jet Jewel, who had been winless in six starts as a racehorse. It's uncertain whether the decision to buy back Jewel's Reward was influenced by business sense or emotion, but Mrs. Graham was certainly rewarded. Jewel's Reward earned $349,642 in 1957, then a record for a two-year-old.

An incident involving Jewel's Reward once provoked

Mrs. Graham to show that her own employees weren't the only people whose jobs might be in jeopardy when she was on the scene.

After Jewel's Reward was disqualified in the 1958 Flamingo, she tried unsuccessfully to get the stewards fired. "I found it somewhat ironic that later in the winter the Florida turf writers voted the lady an award as the best sportsman of the year," said Keene Daingerfield, one of the stewards.

The '58 Flamingo was an awkward experience for Mrs. Graham. The stewards posted the inquiry sign immediately after the race—"and the decision was one of the easiest I have ever had to make," Daingerfield once recalled. "Had the interference been half or even a third as bad, the number would have had to come down."

With the result not official, Mrs. Graham and her party made their way to the presentation area in the infield. Whether they were encouraged or discouraged to do so by Hialeah Park personnel is unclear, but there they all were— Mrs. Graham and company—in the infield waiting for the stewards to rule on the race. Also waiting was the Florida governor, who was there to award the winner a trophy. During the wait, Mrs. Graham was photographed, as were Jewel's Reward, jockey Manny Ycaza, and trainer Ivan Parke.

The incident was made all the worse because the horse moved up to first on the disqualification was Tim Tam, owned by Mrs. Gene Markey of Calumet Farm.

It has been written that Mrs. Graham and Mrs. Markey were feuding in 1958. Mrs. Graham reportedly had tried to hire away Calumet Farm trainer Ben Jones. But she wouldn't have been the only owner who attempted to obtain Jones' services as a trainer. As Margaret Glass pointed out near the end of her long tenure as Calumet Farm secretary and treasurer, "nothing as exciting as a feud" existed between the two women. "Rivalry would certainly

*Mrs. Elizabeth Arden Graham (right) and Mrs. Warren Wright, who
later remarried, becoming Mrs. Gene Markey. Their stables sometimes
competed against each other. (Courtesy Keeneland-Cook)*

have been a more appropriate way of expressing it. There was no real animosity between Mrs. Graham and Mrs. Markey; although their horses may have been rivals—that doesn't mean anything that grievous necessarily in the horse business."

However, Melvin Cinnamon had quit as manager for Mrs. Graham at her Maine Chance Farm in the fall of 1957 and had gone to work at Calumet on January 1, 1958. "Since Mrs. Graham didn't want to lose Melvin and when he quit he did decide to come here, no doubt she was even more displeased when her colt's number came down to a Calumet horse," explained Mrs. Glass.

In 1982, Edwin Pope of the *Miami Herald* wrote of the 1958 disqualification: "Mrs. Markey was so distraught for Mrs. Graham that she asked for a private trophy presentation in the directors' room. President Eisenhower's wife Mamie sent Mrs. Graham a sympathy telegram. At least, when her number came down and her face turned the traditional Flamingo pink, Mrs. Graham had the cosmetics to cover it."

Mrs. Graham, who was cheered by the crowd, "returned to the stands with dignity and grace, winning the respect of all," according to one story. Another account described her as "smiling, but with tears in her eyes," as she "watched the $97,000 purse go to her arch rival." Crossing the track, Mrs. Graham met up with Calumet trainer H. A. ("Jimmy") Jones and, offering her congratulations, shook hands with him.

Parke, her trainer, recalled that the post-race incident was "embarrassing, very embarrassing for that lady. But she held her head high and she went through it real good. She never said one word about it—never in all the time I was with her."

Although Mrs. Graham had a reputation as a difficult, de-manding owner, Parke had nothing but good things to say about his tenure at Maine Chance. "I don't know anything about the other people," he said, "but she treated me real nice. I had a real good relationship with her. She loved the animals. She really loved her horses. The morning that I told her I was leaving, she cried. She was one of the nicest persons that I ever trained for."

Jewel's Reward ran in the 1958 Derby, a race that also attracted the ballyhooed West Coast stretch run. ri Silky Sullivan. Mrs. Graham paid the handsome horse a surprise social call at his Churchill Downs stall during Derby Week. "He's lovely," she said, offering Silky several lumps of sugar. "He's magnificent. What a fine-looking animal."

Mrs. Graham was enthusiastic about racing, and one morning when Jewel's Reward worked out extremely early before the Derby, trainer Ivan Parke wasn't able to get the Maine Chance owner into the Churchill Downs stands to watch her horse. So this lady in her 70s observed the workout while standing on top of a car parked in the stable area.

Jewel's Reward and stablemate Ebony Pearl were favored in the Derby, but both colts finished out of the money. Jewel's Reward ran fourth while Ebony Pearl, who tried to take a bite out of a horse as the field turned for home, wound up tenth.

Jewel's Reward was a biter, too. So the story goes, he once bit Mrs. Graham's finger while she was feeding him sugar. "That's the only Arden employee who ever bit her back," somebody wisecracked.

12

Diary of a Derby Winner

JANUARY 18—RAINDROPS KEEP FALLING IN CALIFORNIA. If the rains don't stop soon, the state is an odds-on favorite to be washed away into the Pacific.

A reporter from Louisville calls trainer Laz Barrera in California and asks him for a report on Affirmed, the champion two-year-old colt of 1977. It turns out that Affirmed is doing just fine, but, because of the rains, the Florida-bred colt hasn't been making much progress in his training.

"He's doing very well," Barrera says, speaking from his stable at Santa Anita Park. "He hasn't been training too much because we got rain here for so long and the main track has been most of the time closed."

Barrera says it didn't rain yesterday but that it had rained for twenty-seven or twenty-eight straight days before that.

Barrera says he had planned on bringing Affirmed out for his three-year-old debut on February 8 in the San Vicente Stakes but now that race might be out of the question for the Harbor View Farm colt. "I'm way behind schedule with him because no way I can train him with the way it's been raining here," Barrera says.

Has the colt developed over the winter? "Yeah, he got bigger and he grow up a little bit more."

What about the Kentucky Derby? "Long way off. I think he's a very good contender for the Derby but you are in

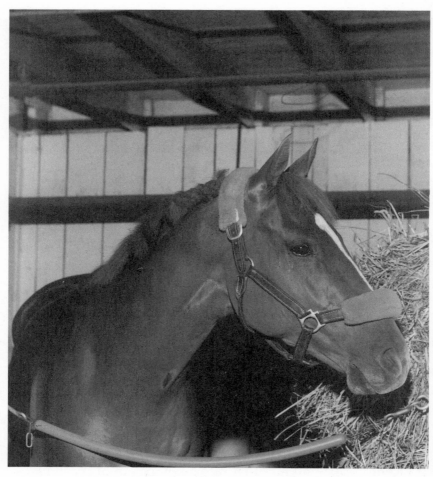

Affirmed at Churchill Downs. (Photo by Dick Martin, Louisville, Kentucky)

January, the race is in May—we're six months away from that."

Not quite six months. Less than four months, to be exact. And the countdown has begun.

March 1—Six weeks later, and Affirmed still has yet to race this year. The reporter from Kentucky calls Barrera again and asks him about a note in the *Daily Racing Form* indicating that the trainer might leave California with Affirmed.

"Well, you know, you don't believe everything what these people say," Barrera says. "I don't talk to nobody and tell them I leave or no leave. I been telling everybody I'm gonna run couple of races here, then go to the Wood Memorial. Don't listen to the rumors because all the time when there's a good horse, the rumors are around."

Barrera says that he plans to give Affirmed four races leading up to the Kentucky Derby—a 6½-furlong allowance on March 8, the San Felipe on March 18, the Santa Anita Derby on April 2, and the Wood Memorial on April 22.

"He been working very good," Barrera says of Affirmed.

What about the weather? "Last night we got five inches of rain here."

Wonder if Santa Claus brought Barrera a supply of umbrellas for Christmas?

March 8—Affirmed finally returns to the races, winning by five lengths under Steve Cauthen.

"I never had to set him down," Cauthen says. "He did it all himself. I had to hit him twice just to keep his mind on his business. As he gets seasoning, he'll respond more when I hit him. Today, I just let him know the race wasn't over. He's just right."

Barrera says he's "very satisfied" with the race. "I was glad to get a race into him. Now, he's right on schedule."

March 16—Two days before the San Felipe, Barrera says that Affirmed is doing great. "He's training well, and he's coming along as we've scheduled for him."

Affirmed will be ridden in the San Felipe by Cauthen, who has obtained an injunction to stay a five-day suspension that would have put him on the sidelines for the race.

March 18—Affirmed wins the San Felipe by two lengths over Chance Dancer. "When Chance Dancer came up, Affirmed was just waiting and then he really took off," Cauthen says.

Barrera again is satisfied. "I'm pleased with his stamina," the trainer says. "Now I know he can go any distance. He'll run two miles."

But not everybody is satisfied.

One racing observer in California tells sports columnist Mike Barry of *The Louisville Times*: "I thought Affirmed was life-and-death, Cauthen really had to get into him to get by that other horse [Chance Dancer] in the stretch."

Chance Dancer is no Kentucky Derby horse. "Can't drag him a mile and a quarter," Barry says.

"And yet Chance Dancer had Affirmed as straight as a string," the California man tells Barry. "In the winner's circle, Affirmed looked to me like a tired horse, a mighty tired horse."

Hmmm.

March 31—Steve Cauthen's suspension, which was stayed for the San Felipe, is in effect for the Santa Anita Derby. So Barrera has decided to use a coin flip to determine whether Laffit Pincay, Jr., or Angel Cordero, Jr., will ride Affirmed in the big race.

The coin comes up tails, making Pincay the winner.

April 1—Alydar wins the Florida Derby by two lengths over Believe It. "Alydar is a standout right now," says W. C.

("Woody") Stephens, trainer of Believe It. "But I can run with any of the rest of 'em."

Stephens doesn't sing the praises of Affirmed.

"He's not going to get nothing," Stephens says. "He's been wintering in California. They had such a terrible winter out there, and Barrera has had to miss so many days of training with Affirmed."

Stephens opines that Affirmed "may get beat" in the Santa Anita Derby tomorrow.

"I don't think California horses compare with these kind of horses," Stephens adds. "There have been a couple of horses come out of California and win the Derby, but more horses come out of Hialeah and Gulfstream."

April 2—Affirmed wins the Santa Anita Derby by eight lengths.

"The moment the big chestnut streaked across the finish line, 48,066 admirers in Big Orange Country went wild," writes sports editor Dick Fenlon of *The Louisville Times.* "Laz Barrera reached out and pulled Steve Cauthen into his arms, enclosing the dimpled darling in a hearty Cuban bear hug.

"The smiles on their faces started somewhere near Pasadena and ran concurrently to Long Beach. Affirmed, the orange-hued blazer, was one giant step closer to the showdown that the horse world is awaiting—the East vs. West Kentucky Derby—Alydar against Affirmed, and may the best horse win."

How did Cauthen like the view from the box seats instead of the view behind Affirmed's neck?

"It's different," the young jockey says, "but I was glad to see him win and glad to see him come out of the race good."

Pincay raves over Affirmed. "This horse has every chance to be one of the great ones, like Secretariat and Sham,"

Pincay says. "A horse this good makes you feel like a really great jockey because they do it all so easily."

Affirmed's victory should answer all questions regarding whether the winter rains in Southern California had ruined Barrera's training schedule.

"He's ready," Barrera says. "He's right where I want him to be. I only had 45 days to get him ready for this race because of all the rain, and I was worried about rushing him. But he showed today that he's the same horse he was as a 2-year-old—probably better."

Despite Affirmed's victory, the critics find reason to fault the way the colt is being brought up to the Kentucky Derby because Barrera now has changed his mind regarding the colt's next race. Instead of sending him east, Barrera has decided to give Affirmed his final prep for the Kentucky Derby in the Hollywood Derby on April 16.

This decision might be a mistake, some observers believe. After a bit of research, one reporter soon will write that in the past quarter of a century seven Kentucky Derby winners raced earlier in their three-year-old seasons in California (Hill Gail, Determine, Swaps, Tomy Lee, Lucky Debonair, Majestic Prince, and Bold Forbes), and they all had one thing in common: Each shipped east to get at least one prep under his belt before running for the roses.

Barrera is an astute trainer—maybe the best in the business—and he should know what's best for his horse. He explains that he doesn't want to fly the colt from California to New York for the Wood Memorial and then to Louisville for the Derby. Too much traveling. Moreover, Barrera notes that Affirmed likes the Hollywood Park track, the colt having won there in fast time as a two-year-old.

Knowledgeable racing people respect Barrera for being the great trainer that he is, but certain ones still wonder whether he has erred by keeping Affirmed in California.

Only time will tell.

April 8—Affirmed gives Barrera the scare of his life. He bucks his exercise boy off and runs the wrong way on the racetrack before veering into the stable area and heading for Barrera's barn. Luckily, this valuable colt doesn't hurt himself.

"Believe me, I thought I was going to have a heart attack," Barrera says. "He's usually a kind colt. Do anything you ask him to. He was just so full of himself, that's all."

April 15—Talking to two reporters from Louisville who arrived this morning at his Hollywood Park barn, Barrera says he hasn't seen Alydar in any of the colt's three-year-old races, not even on television. "I saw enough of him last year," Barrera says. "I have to worry about my horse. Horses are like women. You have to worry about your wife. You can't worry about somebody else's wife."

At the training track, Barrera and the reporters watch Affirmed gallop. "Look at the way that sucker gallops," Barrera says. Affirmed looks like a picture horse, and on the way back to the barn, one reporter comments to his colleague that Affirmed is the best-looking horse he's seen since Secretariat.

Later in the day in the Hollywood Park jockeys' quarters, Cauthen discusses Affirmed and tomorrow's Hollywood Derby. "He's coming up to this race great," Cauthen says. "He's really feeling good, doing good, looking good."

April 16—Cauthen's instructions from Barrera for the Hollywood Derby are to go to the lead—and the whip. "I tell him, 'Don't take no chances,'" Barrera later says. "I say, 'Go to the lead and don't let nobody get ahead.' And I tell him, 'Use the whip. Don't let him start fooling around when he get the lead.'"

Cauthen hits Affirmed twelve times coming down the homestretch, but the colt doesn't draw away to a widening victory. He wins by two lengths. The race leaves press box observers with different opinions. Some like it, some don't, and some aren't sure what to make of it.

"He didn't respond a lot to being hit," Cauthen says at a press conference afterward, "but if some horses came up to him, I'm sure he'd dig in and go ahead. I knew he was the best horse. When he's hooking a horse, you don't have to hit him. He fights back then. But when he's in front by himself, he sort of eases himself up. Beating the heck out of him doesn't do much good."

His time for the mile and one-eighth on a fast track is 1:48 1/5. Nothing special.

Affirmed's detractors point out that his slow-motion time of 13 1/5 seconds for the final furlong compares poorly with Alydar's final eighth of 11 3/5 seconds in the Florida Derby.

Of course, after running as fast as he did early in the Hollywood Derby—22 2/5 seconds for the first quarter, 45 seconds for the half, 1:09 2/5 for six furlongs—Affirmed couldn't have been expected to have enough in reserve to come through with a dynamite closing eighth.

Cauthen is asked at the press conference to comment on this business of Alydar's and Affirmed's closing eighths. "Everybody sees into it their own theory," Cauthen says, "but I was very pleased with my own horse and I'm glad I'm on him."

One California writer points out, rather bluntly: "Some people are saying you'll fold under the Derby pressure."

"We'll find out May whatever it is," Cauthen replies. "I hope I'm up to it. I think I will be."

Jockey Darrel McHargue speaks highly of Affirmed after finishing third behind him aboard Radar Ahead.

"I haven't seen Alydar run, but from what I've seen of Affirmed, he's an exceptional racehorse," McHargue says. "He's smart, he takes care of himself and he knows how to run. If Alydar is going to beat him, he definitely better have his running shoes on."

At a press conference after the race, Harbor View Farm owner Louis Wolfson whispers to Billy Reed, sports editor of *The Courier-Journal* in Louisville, to ask Barrera about a story appearing a week earlier in the *Los Angeles Times*. A writer stated that according to racetrack rumors, Barrera and Wolfson had accepted an under-the-table payment from Hollywood Park to keep Affirmed in California instead of shipping him east to receive his final Kentucky Derby prep.

Wolfson obviously is indignant about the story, and he wants the matter brought out in the open. Reed asks Barrera about the story, and the trainer reacts angrily.

"Rumors," Barrera snorts. "I'm surprised that a man would print rumors. Why don't he print who gave him the rumors? Then we could sue him. Nobody can buy me for under-the-table money. That horse won $174,000 today. That is plenty of money on top of the table.

"Here I have a horse that is going to earn me more money than any horse ever has and I'm going to sell him for money under the table? That is silly. I'm going to do what is best for my horse. I don't got to travel my horse all over the country to please a writer. I got to please my owner."

Wolfson also speaks his mind.

"I've never been a freeloader," he says. "Every racetrack in the country has offered Harbor View Farm money or free hotel rooms, lots of things, to ship horses in, but I always pay my own way. We've been in this business 19 years and we've been in the top five in both racing and breeding, and everything we do is above the table."

April 23—Following a flight from California, Affirmed arrives in Louisville during late afternoon. Accompanying him on the trip are groom Juan Alaniz, exercise boy Jose Ithier, and night watchman Thomas Martinez. Larry Barrera, son of the trainer, is already in Louisville to greet

Affirmed, who is bedded down in Barn 41 at Churchill Downs.

April 29—As Affirmed steps on the Churchill Downs track at 8:15 A.M., the sky is dotted with hot-air balloons competing in the Derby Festival Balloon Race.

The colt works a mile and an eighth in 1:56¹/₅. On the way back to the barn, Laz Barrera sees something gleaming in the soil. He stops and picks up a dime. To Barrera, this is a good omen. "A heads-up dime," Barrera says, showing it to a companion before putting it in his jacket pocket. "When you do something good, you get lucky."

The workout receives mixed reactions. Some wonder why it wasn't any faster. Yet, Barrera is pleased with the effort.

"Everybody said it was very slow, very slow," Barrera later would recall. "He don't impress nobody. But he work around the turn from the seven-eighths pole to the three-quarter pole, and he went the last eighth in 12 [¹/₅]. There are not too many horses that can do that on a very cuppy track. Nobody appreciate how good that work was."

One topic of conversation around Louisville deals with the wagering. Whose handsome nose will the bettors put more money on in the Derby—Alydar or Affirmed?

Mike Battaglia, the program linemaker at Churchill Downs, says it will be Alydar. But not by much.

"I'm not taking anything away from Affirmed because I think he's a helluva horse, but you have to favor one of them and I've got to go with Alydar as the program favorite."

Why?

"That's tough to say," Battaglia replies. "I know that Affirmed beat Alydar in four of their six races last year, but Alydar's races this year have been more impressive than Affirmed's.

"Also, their styles of running are a factor, Alydar's off-the-pace style as opposed to Affirmed's front-running style. Plus the fact that Alydar has raced in Kentucky—in the Blue Grass Stakes—and people here have seen him run. And you have that stigma of horses coming here from the West Coast."

April 30—My Derby selections appear in *The Courier-Journal* today, with Alydar ranked first and Affirmed second.

At the barn this morning, Barrera calls me off to the side and, in a quiet way, lets me know that he was surprised and disappointed that I would rank Alydar ahead of Affirmed. I am taken aback, because Laz Barrera has forgotten more about racing than I'll ever know and I didn't think he could possibly take my selections seriously. I try to soothe Barrera, but he has his pride, his Latin pride, and I have wounded him.

(Barrera would get over his hurt and, in time, would poke fun at me. He delighted in telling people this story: "Jeeem Bolus, he call me all winter when I am in California and ask me how my horse ees doing. I tell him Affirmed ees doing fine. Jeeem come out to California and watch Affirmed ween the Hollywood Derby. He see for himself that the horse ees doing fine. But when Jeeem come back to Kentucky and he hear the band play 'My Old Kentucky Home,' he peeek a Kentucky horse—Calumet Farm's Alydar.")

May 2—Standing outside Barn 41, Barrera is interviewed by the press.

Question: Affirmed is an easy horse to ride, isn't he?
Answer: He's easy to do anything with.

Question: Would you think that John Veitch will tell his rider to try to blow on by your horse with Alydar and not try to hook him?

Answer: Yeah, but he no got a jet plane that can go blow by my horse.

Question: Your horse has never had Bute, has he?
Answer: No.

Question: And he won't have Bute for the Derby?
Answer: He don't need it. You take aspirin if you don't got a headache?

A reporter then comments that most everybody in the Affirmed camp seems to characterize the colt as "a fighter."

"You might beat him," Barrera says. "Look, any champion been beat. But you have to be bleeding to beat him. He's a competitor. When he goes in there, he give everything that he got."

Mr. and Mrs. Louis Wolfson visit Spendthrift Farm in Lexington, Kentucky, where they receive satisfaction from looking at three stallions in particular—Raise a Native, Exclusive Native, and Majestic Prince, each of whom will have a son race in the Derby.

As a matter of fact, the three top contenders in the Derby all trace to Raise a Native, who raced for Wolfson's Harbor View Farm. Raise a Native won all four of his starts in 1963 before his career was cut short by an injury.

Affirmed, an Exclusive Native colt bred by Wolfson, is a grandson of Raise a Native. Alydar is a son of Raise a Native. Sensitive Prince is a son of Majestic Prince.

It's quite satisfying for Wolfson to know that Raise a Native has had such an impact on this year's Derby.

May 3—Barrera sharpens Affirmed up with a five-furlong workout in a lively 59 seconds. The colt goes the first quarter in $24^2/_5$ seconds and the half in $47^1/_5$ seconds. He completes the drill with a final furlong in $11^4/_5$ seconds.

Barrera likes what he sees. He knows his horse is sharp. And in his mind, he knows his horse is going to win the Derby.

He will later recall that after he saw Affirmed's final Derby work, "I said, 'The party is over. Nobody is going to beat this horse.'"

Barrera tells Joe Hirsch of the *Daily Racing Form* that he believes Affirmed deserves to be favored over Calumet Farm's Alydar for the Derby. "I can understand the sentiment for Calumet, but I feel we have the best horse," Barrera says to Hirsch.

Barrera says Affirmed couldn't be more eager now. "He is, in the old Spanish expression, like a man who just got married."

Meanwhile, the Wolfsons are interviewed by the Louisville newspapers. Both talk of what Affirmed means to them.

"Let's put it this way," Wolfson says. "With all the problems of the world and with the frustrations and violence, this horse has reduced some of the problems for me, made me stop worrying about things I can't do much about. He has given me so many pleasing and happy moments. My outlook on life may be better because of him."

Soon after Affirmed's workout, Mrs. Wolfson glances admiringly at the colt back at the barn. "It's a dream come true to have a horse like this," she says. "This is the kind of horse that you endeavor to breed and train and be around."

Mrs. Wolfson has been associated with horses her whole life. Her father was the late Hirsch Jacobs, one of the greatest trainers of all time.

"My father would have loved this horse," she says.

Mrs. Wolfson knows a good horse when she sees one. And every time she sees Affirmed, her eyes light up. She loves being around the colt.

"I think he knows my high-pitched voice," Mrs. Wolfson says after going over and speaking affectionately to Affirmed, who is standing inside his stall at Churchill Downs. "I think that he likes attention. He knows he's special. I know he knows he's special."

Just then, Affirmed begins tossing his head around. He realizes that it's feeding time, and he is eager to go about the business of cleaning up his feed tub.

"You love to see a horse do that," Mrs. Wolfson says. "He's alert, he's bright. You would never know he worked."

Mrs. Wolfson describes Affirmed as a natural athlete. "He loves to run," she says.

Mrs. Wolfson, a petite blonde, has owned some talented racehorses over the years, including Hail to Reason, the 1960 juvenile champion. Of all the horses that have represented her, Affirmed holds a special place in her heart. "He's become my favorite," Mrs. Wolfson says. "Being around so many great horses, I just feel I haven't been around one like him. He's a very, very unusual Thoroughbred."

Mrs. Wolfson is quick to give credit to the entire team that has worked with Affirmed—groom Juan Alaniz, exercise boy Jose Ithier, jockey Steve Cauthen, and trainer Laz Barrera.

"After all the winter rains in California, Lazaro has done a fantastic job getting him ready," she says.

Mrs. Wolfson says that Affirmed and Cauthen work well together. "Steve and Affirmed have a tremendous amount of maturity. Affirmed is like an older horse. Nothing bothers him. Nothing bothers Steve Cauthen. They have a sense of rapport between themselves."

One final comment from Mrs. Wolfson: "I think we're running the best horse Saturday. I think he has the potential to be a great horse."

May 4—On a rainy morning at Churchill Downs, eleven horses are entered in the Derby. "The weather doesn't concern us," Barrera says. "I'm very confident. My horse is perfectly sound. He worked tremendous yesterday, and he's in good shape."

Affirmed draws the No. 2 post position, Alydar No. 10. Two speedsters, Raymond Earl and Sensitive Prince, land in the Nos. 1 and 11 starting spots, respectively.

John Veitch, trainer of Alydar, says that he believes Affirmed's No. 2 post position might pose "a serious problem."

Learning of Veitch's comments, Barrera says he believes the Calumet trainer should train his horse "and let me train mine—and worry about his post position and let mine alone."

Veitch's analysis of Affirmed's post position goes like this: "I think it poses a serious problem to them. They've got to make a decision. They've got two alternatives . . .

No. 1—"To break the horse sharply, let him run into the first turn, get a good position with him and then hope that they can get him to relax after they do it. If they feel confident that they can get him to relax, then there's really no problem at all.

"But if you think about it, he's going to have Raymond Earl right on the inside of him running, and he's going to have probably Sensitive Prince running from the outside. Going into the first turn, three jocks that are riding their horses to get a position, it might pose a serious problem to getting a horse to relax."

No. 2—"They can take him back from the very start and drop in behind the speed horses. Then they'll hope that they can get a good position, that something opens up, and that there won't be a horse or two on the outside of them.

"But if they should get boxed in and Raymond Earl should stop in front of them after going, say, five-eighths or three-quarters of a mile, fall back on Affirmed and that jock [Cauthen] should have to take up, that might be a serious problem. Particularly when you're running against a horse of Alydar's ability. Anything that encumbers your route any little bit can be a very, very serious problem.

"But, of course, it might work out that Jerkens' horse

[Sensitive Prince, trained by Allen Jerkens] and Raymond Earl go right to the lead, Affirmed might just be sitting here, nobody on the outside of him, so he could work his way to the outside of maybe even Alydar when Alydar comes through."

In reply to Veitch's comments, Barrera says: "I don't say how he's going to run his horse or what's going to happen to him. I don't care. He can run any way he wants. I never make any comment about nobody else's horse. It surprises me that a young man like him—and I got a lot of respect for him—makes this kind of comment. That makes me mad. Nobody can tell you what's going to happen leaving the gate.

"The only thing I say all my life is Alydar is a great horse, a *helluva* horse, and a horse you have to run your eyeballs out to beat. But he got a job to do, and I got mine to do."

May 5—The experts make their Derby selections.

Andy Beyer of the *Washington Star* thinks so little of Affirmed that he doesn't even pick him to finish in the top four. Beyer's picks: 1—Alydar, 2—Believe It, 3—Sensitive Prince, 4—Darby Creek Road.

Mike Barry of *The Louisville Times* selects Affirmed to finish first, Alydar second, Believe It third, and Darby Creek Road fourth.

This Derby is billed as the one that has everything.

This Derby has Calumet Farm, the greatest name in the race's long history, and Steve Cauthen, the eighteen-year-old jockey whose career has been nothing short of sensational. Calumet is bidding for its ninth Derby trophy, Cauthen his first.

This Derby has Affirmed and Alydar, two standout colts who are renewing their memorable rivalry of 1977. Affirmed won four of their six meetings last year, but the races were close. After 5⅛ miles of competing against

Alydar in the six races, Affirmed held an overall advantage of about a length.

This Derby has an unbeaten horse, Sensitive Prince, and another solid contender in Believe It. The two colts are trained by Hall of Famers Allen Jerkens and W. C. ("Woody") Stephens, respectively.

A Hollywood movie scriptwriter couldn't have put together a better cast of characters to go with the talented horses in this 104th Derby.

May 6—It's the first Saturday in May. Derby Day.

The gates open at 8 A.M., and the first 131,004 fans head through the turnstiles. The first race is run at 11:30, and the Derby is the eighth race on the card.

At about 4 P.M., a group of reporters spot Barrera near Barn 41. They go over to him, and he talks about the Derby.

"I like to see Sensitive Prince and that other horse [Raymond Earl] go to the lead and I lay third," Barrera said. "Relax behind those two horses. Alydar has to come from behind."

"You look very relaxed," someone told Barrera.

"I tell you why," Barrera replies. "I did all my job. My horse is perfectly sound. Eat everything. Acting good. Very happy this morning. Nothing more I can do. It's out of my hands."

Would he do anything differently with Affirmed if he had it to do over again?

"No, I think I did everything right," Barrera replies.

Later, Barrera says, "I was nervous the whole week. Not today. Today I feel my job is done. I don't feel I've done anything wrong. My horse is sound, sound, sound. He's game. He fight. He give you the last thing inside of him."

Soon the horses are called over for the Kentucky Derby. Shortly, it is post time for the big race.

Trainer Laz Barrera talked with reporters in the Churchill Downs stable area on the afternoon of the 1978 Kentucky Derby. (Photo by Dick Martin, Louisville, Kentucky)

The field is sent on its way at 5:41, and the start is good for all but Special Honor, who rears at the break. Raymond Earl, the speedball ridden by fifty-seven-year-old R. L. Baird, goes to the lead from his starting position on the rail. As the eleven starters thunder past the wire the first time, Sensitive Prince, coming over from his outside post position, is head and head with Affirmed for second place. Alydar is far back.

Going into the first turn, Sensitive Prince moves up and over to the inside, putting Affirmed in slightly crowded conditions. Cauthen, ever alert, promptly takes Affirmed to the outside and out of possible trouble.

Sensitive Prince overtakes Raymond Earl rounding the clubhouse turn, and Affirmed is perfectly placed in third, just where Barrera wants him. Sensitive Prince still leads after six furlongs, but Affirmed moves up on the outside at the far turn. Alydar, meanwhile, is back in eighth place.

Sensitive Prince now is faltering after sizzling through a fast half-mile in 45³/₅ seconds. His jockey, Mickey Solomone, begins to apply the whip around the turn, but the rider's efforts are to no avail. Sensitive Prince is finished.

Affirmed goes to the lead rounding the far turn, but he is to be joined by Believe It, who comes up on the outside in a big move. "When Believe It came to me, we moved together to the head of the lane," Cauthen would later say. "I really didn't ask my horse that much. He just did most of it on his own. Then he opened up a couple of lengths on Believe It. So when he opened a couple of lengths, he started pricking his ears like he always does and that's when I started hitting him."

Cauthen hits Affirmed six times, the first whack coming inside the three-sixteenths pole.

As Affirmed reaches the eighth pole, Believe It is tiring and Alydar now is third on the outside, but he isn't moving fast enough to catch the leader. The message now is coming through loud and clear to the big crowd and a national television audience—Affirmed is going to win the Kentucky Derby.

It's all over but the shouting.

Alydar, feeling the sting of jockey Jorge Velasquez's whip eleven times coming down the long stretch, makes up a lot of ground at the very end, but it's too late. Affirmed wins by a length and a half over Alydar.

The winning time of 2:01$\frac{1}{5}$ ties for the fifth fastest in Derby history.

Affirmed pays $5.60 to win as the second choice behind Alydar.

At a press conference afterward, somebody asks Barrera whether Affirmed might be caught by Alydar in a longer race.

"No, no, no, no, no, no, no," Barrera says, causing the reporters to break up in laughter. "We can go five miles, and it's going to be the same result. Excuses is enough."

What about an earlier move by Alydar? "No, Alydar move early with him, and we beat him. He move from the middle, we beat him. He move from the back, and we beat him. I don't want to hear no more excuses no more."

Barrera then talks about Affirmed. "This is a horse that you can run him any place you want him. You don't have to go to the lead. If you want to use him on the lead, he go to the lead. But he don't have to.

"If you ever take a look the whole week at the horse, he look like he come from the beauty parlor—shining and nothing bothers him.

"I was very confident I was going to win it—against the opinion of most everybody because he run in California. It doesn't matter whether he run in China, he's a very good horse . . . and I'm very proud of my horse."

And Barrera is proud of Cauthen, too. "Steve Cauthen rode the horse perfect."

Spotting this writer, who had picked Alydar to win, Barrera says with a laugh, "I tell you to change your mind."

Laz, some guys are just too hardheaded to listen to good, sound advice.

May 7—Jockey Jorge Velasquez, who rode Alydar in the Derby, said afterward that the Calumet colt was having trouble getting hold of the track in the early part of the race.

Barrera comments on that matter this morning at Barn 41.

"I don't know," Barrera says. "Might be right. Velasquez is a good rider. But if he don't get hold of the track, he don't finish second, either. The only trouble he got, he can not get a hold of Affirmed."

May 8—Affirmed leaves Louisville in the morning, and it's raining.

Raining?

Isn't that the way this story starts out?

It sure does, and Affirmed completes the Derby diary by finding a huge pot of gold at the end of the rainbow.

Owner-breeder E. P. Taylor proudly held Northern Dancer in the winner's circle at the 1964 Kentucky Derby. Trainer Horatio A. Luro stood next to Taylor. Bill Hartack rode Northern Dancer. (Courtesy Churchill Downs Incorporated/Kinetic Corporation)

13

Northern Dancer:
A Derby Winner Who
Left His Mark Forever

NORTHERN DANCER, THE KING OF STALLIONS, was still a kid at heart even when he was in his twenties.

The first thing this internationally known Thoroughbred did when the gate was opened to his paddock on the sprawling acres of Windfields Farm was roll on the ground like a playful youngster, first on his right side and then on his left.

Bright and alert, full of vim and vigor, Northern Dancer quickly bounced up on his feet and took off running up and down alongside the fenceline of the paddock. Up and down, up and down.

A couple of visitors from Kentucky dropped by Windfields in 1983 to take a look at the old boy, but Northern Dancer understandably enough was more interested in something else. Northern Dancer was all worked up because in the distance he saw a van at the loading chute near the breeding barn. The van, he knew, had brought a mare to Windfields. And Northern Dancer, it seemed, had this idea that every mare that arrived at Windfields was a date for him in the breeding barn.

Northern Dancer, you little rascal, you.

If he were a human, he would have been called a dirty old man, but in horsedom the twenty-two-year-old Northern Dancer was known as the world's most influential sire.

Soon he was taken from the paddock and returned to

the barn because, with mares on his mind, he wouldn't calm down while outside.

Northern Dancer once occupied a stall on the other side of the stud barn. Trouble was, he sometimes would stand on his hind feet and put his front hoofs on the wall so that he could look out a window high up in his stall. And, just guess what he could see by looking out that window? The breeding barn, of course.

So Northern Dancer was relocated and forced to take up residence on the opposite side of the stud barn.

When he was out in his paddock, Northern Dancer demonstrated that old drive and enthusiasm. He would sometimes even chase birds. "He's a very active horse," Joe Thomas, Windfields vice-president of Thoroughbred operations, said in 1983.

A visitor couldn't help but notice that the proud Northern Dancer, with his head held high, gave off the impression that he was aware that he was something special. Indeed, he was something very special, this 1964 Kentucky Derby winner, this father of champion racehorses, this sire whose blood was in such great demand.

With those kinds of credentials, Northern Dancer obviously didn't lack for attention at Windfields. "He's the one that makes all the wheels turn and he gets treated accordingly," said Joe Hickey, administrative manager for Windfields Farm in Maryland.

Northern Dancer was looking just fine when we visited him in Maryland. Sure, he hadn't defied Father Time completely. He had a slight sway in his back, but for the most part he appeared and acted like a younger horse.

"He's always been a very good-feeling horse," Hickey said. "He's got a lot of spunk and spirit to him, and he looks great. We're very pleased with him."

Northern Dancer recognized people. Hickey said that Mrs. E. P. Taylor, wife of the Windfields Farm founder, would go into the barn and Northern Dancer would know her. "Of course, Mrs. Taylor would always bring him sugar when she came to see him, and he would come to expect it, too," Hickey said.

Northern Dancer once grabbed Mrs. Taylor. "He got ahold of her finger," Thomas said, "and if one of our best horsemen hadn't been right there by him and been able to get him loose, there's no telling how much damage he would have done."

Northern Dancer was one of seventeen members of Windfields' blue-blooded stallion fraternity in 1983. Halo (the sire of 1983 Kentucky Derby winner Sunny's Halo and later 1989 Derby champion Sunday Silence) grazed close by in the paddock right next to Northern Dancer's. European classic winner Assert, a grandson of Northern Dancer, kicked up his heels and romped around as a next-door neighbor on the other side of Northern Dancer's paddock. And down the way just a bit, on the other side of Assert's paddock, was The Minstrel, a son of Northern Dancer.

The four horses in that line of paddocks—Halo, Northern Dancer, Assert, and The Minstrel—represented horse-flesh valued in excess of $100 million.

Breeding is a high-priced business, and the biggest dollars spent in the yearling market for years have gone for the Northern Dancer sire line.

Northern Dancer, the leading sire in England/Ireland for four years (1970, 1977, 1983, and 1984), made more of an impact on European racing circles than he did in the United States. He is the only Kentucky Derby winner to sire a winner of the 1½-mile Epsom Derby, a race with global prestige. As a matter of fact, Northern Dancer sired three Epsom Derby winners—Nijinsky II in 1970, The Minstrel in 1977, and Secreto in 1983. Nijinsky II was voted European Horse of the Year in 1970, and The Minstrel was acclaimed 1977's Horse of the Year in England.

Of the eleven highest prices in the history of the

prestigious Keeneland July Selected Yearling Sale, seven were sired by Northern Dancer and three by Nijinsky II.

In 1982, at Keeneland, the British Bloodstock Agency (Ireland) acquired a son of Nijinsky II for $4.25 million, a world's record at the time. In 1981 at Keeneland, essentially the same BBA syndicate set the previous record by paying $3.5 million for a Northern Dancer colt consigned by Windfields Farm. Two other sons of Northern Dancer rang up prices of $3.3 million and $2.95 million, respectively, in 1981. Those two also were sold at Keeneland.

Sheikh Mohammed bin Rashid al Maktoum was beaten out in the bidding for the $4.25-million yearling in 1982 and the $3.5-million yearling in 1981. But the sheikh hasn't always lost when he's gone after the Northern Dancer blood. His Aston Upthorpe Stud broke open its piggy bank to come up with the needed money for the Northern Dancer yearling that sold for the $3.3-million price in 1981. "It's good blood," the sheikh said of the Northern Dancer line. "If you want to breed, you need this blood."

Commenting on his $3.3-million purchase, the sheikh said: "I am very pleased. This is a fine horse."

A fine horse, indeed. The colt, Shareef Dancer (consigned by Windfields Farm) was honored as the champion three-year-old in Europe, England, and Ireland, and his syndication value was a record $40 million.

In 1983, a son of Northern Dancer out of My Bupers sold for a world's-record $10.2 million at the Keeneland July Selected Yearling Sale. That record lasted two years until a son of Nijinsky II out of My Charmer brought $13.1 million at the Keeneland summer auction.

While all too many lines weaken from generation to generation, the Northern Dancer line "just seems to go from strength to strength," in the words of Hickey.

Nearctic, the father of Northern Dancer, sired 49 stakes winners. Northern Dancer sired 145 stakes winners, a record that stood until it was broken in the summer of 1992 by Nijinsky II, who was put down earlier that spring on April 15. Northern Dancer later had his 146th stakes winner, but through late 1993 Nijinsky II had 147 to his credit, and he likely will have even more added-money winners by the time his last runners complete their careers.

Nijinsky II, who was twenty-five at the time of his death, stood his entire career at Claiborne Farm, just outside Paris, Kentucky. One of his sons, Ferdinand, won the 1986 Kentucky Derby, and that same year another colt sired by him, Shahrastani, captured the Epsom Derby.

Nijinsky II, an $84,000 yearling purchased by Charles Engelhard, in 1970 became the first horse in thirty-five years to win the English Triple Crown (St. Leger Stakes, Epsom Derby, and Two Thousand Guineas). "By and large," Hickey said, "it was because of Nijinsky's success in Europe that the very best of Northern Dancer's yearlings were siphoned off to Europe year after year after year."

Nijinsky II's European success stamped Northern Dancer in that part of the world as a success early in his stud career. "That's where all the money was at the time and even to this day," Hickey said in 1988. "So the top dollar came from Europe and the Middle Eastern countries, and that's where the top Northern Dancers went. That, I think, explains best of all the disproportionate number of stakes winners in Europe as opposed to the United States."

Northern Dancer sired only one Kentucky Derby starter, Giboulee, who finished seventh in 1977. In 1982, however, Northern Dancer did have two grandsons—Derby future-book favorite Timely Writer and the highly regarded Hostage—on the grounds at Churchill Downs preparing for the classic, but unfortunately neither colt made it to the post.

Northern Dancer, a small horse, frequently "stamped" his most talented sons and daughters. That is, he passed on his features such as shape, size, and color.

Nijinsky II, however, was an exception. Thomas noted that Nijinsky II took after his mother, Flaming Page, "who was a big, kind of a rough kind of a mare."

Northern Dancer, a bay, had white on the lower part of three legs and a stripe that came down and angled into his left nostril. The Minstrel, who stood just slightly taller than Northern Dancer, also had a stripe that came down and curled over, covering his left nostril. In addition, he had two full white stockings, a three-quarter stocking, and white to well above his ankle on his other leg. "The Minstrel's the spitting image of Northern Dancer, except he's a chestnut," said Thomas, an extremely knowledgeable horseman. "Northern Dancer may be a little bit longer, but other than that, their muscling, their heads, they're almost identical.

"Many of Northern Dancer's get are replicas of him," added Thomas. "He gets a few that are unlike him, but the ones that bring the most money and the ones that are the most popular are the ones that look like him."

Northern Dancer was proof that brilliant racehorses can come in small packages. Back when he ran in the Derby, he was a full four inches shorter than Hill Rise, the favorite. Northern Dancer, the second choice ridden by Bill Hartack, won the Derby in track-record time of 2:00, holding off a late surge by Hill Rise.

Afterward, Jim Murray of the *Los Angeles Times* wrote, "Northern Dancer is the kind of a colt who, if you saw him in your living room, you'd send for a trap and put cheese in it. He's so little, a cat would chase him. But he's so plucky, there's barely room in him for his heart. His legs are barely long enough to keep his tail off the ground. He probably takes a hundred more strides than anyone else in the race, but he's harder to pass up than a third martini."

In retirement, Northern Dancer had a number of breeding sessions with mares taller than he was, particularly at the beginning of his stud career. "In the early days, everybody thought, well, since Northern Dancer was small they wanted to send him a great, big mare," Thomas told us on our visit. "You don't get as many big mares now as in the past. Now people feel that that's really not necessary."

Taller mares presented a problem for Northern Dancer, who had trouble reaching them. Windfields improvised in order to accommodate Northern Dancer. The Windfields barn formerly used for breeding purposes had a tanbark floor. "We dug a hole and the mare could stand down in the hole and then he could mount her," Thomas said.

Windfields later had a breeding barn with an artificial surface, and when a tall mare was brought in, a portable platform—or sort of a "pitcher's mound"—was used for Northern Dancer to stand on.

"He'll scare you to death when he breeds," said Thomas, who vowed during the 1983 breeding season that he would never again watch Northern Dancer breed. "He stands straight up and he gets up there and you think he's going to fall over backwards, which he has in the past. But he's pretty good now; he's pretty agile."

The most mares Northern Dancer ever was bred to in one season was forty-six. Thomas, who died in 1984 after managing Northern Dancer's stud career for most of the stallion's life, could have bred him to considerably more mares. "But I think that I would hurt both him physically, and I'd certainly hurt the market for them because you'd flood the market," Thomas said in 1983. "And also when you start getting up to 50, 60, 70 mares, the quality of the mares has got to drop off because there just aren't that many mares to go around."

Northern Dancer's stud fee started off at 10,000 (Canadian) dollars live foal guaranteed for the 1965–68 seasons. He kept turning out the runners, and his fee kept climbing higher and higher. He was in such demand that there was at least one season to change hands for an astounding $1 million (no guarantee) on the open market.

These fees were paid for a stallion whose breeding itself in 1960 was a bit of a coincidence. That year, his dam, Natalma, a daughter of Native Dancer, was training impressively for the Kentucky Oaks, but she fractured her knee. "We were undecided what to do," Thomas said. "It was a question whether we were going to do surgery on her and bring her back or breed her. We had had another filly by Native Dancer the previous year that had come up with the same problem. We did surgery on her, and it didn't work. In other words, we weren't able to bring her back.

"So we just kicked it around and said, 'Oh, what the hell, why don't we breed her to Nearctic and if she gets in foal, okay; if she doesn't get in foal, then maybe we'll do the surgery and try to bring her back.' So by the time we got her back to Canada and got her bred, it was almost the end of June."

Natalma was the last mare bred to Nearctic that year. Both parents of Northern Dancer were in their first season of breeding. With the gestation period for mares lasting 11 months, Northern Dancer wasn't born until May 27 of the following year, making him a very late foal.

As a yearling, he was offered to prospective buyers for $25,000 at one of Taylor's pre-priced sales in Canada. There were no takers, so Taylor kept the little fellow.

A suggestion was made to geld Northern Dancer, but Taylor rejected that idea and Northern Dancer remained all-man. He was all-racehorse, too. He was the champion three-year-old colt of 1964, winning the Preakness as well as the Derby, both races coming before he actually turned three years of age.

Not only was he rejected by prospective buyers, but Northern Dancer was cast aside as a Kentucky Derby mount by Bill Shoemaker. After winning the Flamingo and Florida Derby aboard Northern Dancer, Shoemaker elected to switch mounts and take Hill Rise in the Kentucky Derby.

Murray wrote that it wasn't hard to imagine why Shoe-maker chose Hill Rise over Northern Dancer. "You wouldn't pick Northern Dancer over a burro if you placed them side-by-side," Murray declared. "You'd want your money back if you drew him at a Griffith Park riding academy. He doesn't look big enough to keep up with the traffic on a bridle path."

Trained throughout his career by master horseman Horatio A. Luro, Northern Dancer was voted Canadian Horse of the Year in 1964 and retired with fourteen victories in eighteen starts.

"One of the great qualities he had was this ability to accelerate," Thomas said. "In the Derby, he's sitting in there and when the hole opened up, Hartack said go. He just stepped on it, and he was gone. That faculty is what has made Northern Dancer and his offspring, too, go a lot farther than people thought that they should, because everybody thought he was basically a miler or something like that. But he had this ability to accelerate and you could rate him, and that's the same way with many of his sons."

Taylor, who bred Northern Dancer and owned him during his racing career, received plenty of advice years ago from folks who bred horses in Kentucky. Some of the advice was good. Some of it wasn't, particularly from those who spoke disparagingly about breeding horses in Canada. Certain Kentucky hardboots told Taylor, "What have you got up there in Canada? You got snow and ice. There's no way you can breed a good horse there."

All Taylor did in Canada was breed such champions as Northern Dancer, Nijinsky II, The Minstrel, and many other outstanding horses.

Northern Dancer stood in Canada for his first four seasons at stud (1965–68). In December of 1968, he was moved to the Windfields operation in Maryland. "We were getting some pretty good mares, but there was a certain amount of resistance to send good mares to Canada,"

Thomas explained. "Canada's always got the reputation of being up north in the Eskimo country and things like that. Mr. Taylor just felt that really Northern Dancer belonged in the United States, where he would have access to better mares.

"We wanted to continue to manage him. He was still our horse. If we had sent him to Kentucky to one of the big farms there, they would have wanted to take over the management of him. We felt that Maryland was convenient enough that anybody that had a good mare in Kentucky or anyplace else would send her to Maryland because there wasn't the same resistance about being that far north."

In 1983, E. P. Taylor's son, Charles, the president of Windfields, recalled Northern Dancer's years in Canada: "Windfields didn't have all that many great mares in those days, nothing like we have now. We sent him some of our best, but they were, compared to what he's getting now, nothing. And a few people shipped up some decent mares from the United States. But he didn't have a very, very strong book for the first seven or eight years, even when he moved to Maryland. Certainly, the last seven or eight years he's had really top books."

At the age of nine, Northern Dancer was syndicated in August of 1970. "He and Nijinsky were syndicated within 48 hours of each other," Hickey said.

Northern Dancer was syndicated for $2.4 million, thirty-two shares at $75,000 each. "He was probably one of the greatest bargains ever as far as a stallion was concerned," Hickey said, "because he was already a proven sire at that point. Nijinsky had already won the Triple Crown."

Nijinsky II, a winner in eleven of thirteen career races, was syndicated for $5.44 million, a world's record that stood until Secretariat broke it in 1973 at $6.08 million.

In the early 1980s, Northern Dancer was getting up there in age, but he was still worth millions. Many millions. In the fall of 1981, a staggering offer of $40 million was

Merry Christmas from a
Christmas past

2009

© UFS

2009

Merry Christmas from a
Christmas past

© UFS

made for Northern Dancer, then already twenty years old. The initial telex that Windfields received came from Horse France, which said it was acting for Dr. Lazlo Urban, a French veterinarian.

"We never had voice contact with him," said Charles Taylor. "It was all done by telex, and he would not tell us who he was acting for, where the horse would stand. But his Telex in English said he was offering 40 million for *the whole horse*, which we took to mean all 32 shares. Joe Thomas telexed back, asking for more details, which were not forthcoming. After we had polled the syndicate, Joe informed Horse France that we could not deliver the horse—much to our relief. We never heard from him again. There was a majority of votes for selling the horse, but there was a significant minority that said they didn't want to sell and some of them were quite adamant about it, just as some of the people who wanted to sell were adamant."

Taylor said that he met Urban after the Prix de l'Arc de Triomphe in Paris in the fall of 1982. "He introduced himself to me, and I said, 'I suppose you can't tell me who your people were.' And he said, 'No.' And I said, 'Can you tell me where the horse would have moved to if you had gotten him?' He said, 'Kentucky.' Which is what we suspected all along. We always assumed it was Kentucky, although I don't know who. He wouldn't tell me who."

Taylor was quoted in a story in December 1982 as saying that he hoped when the end came for Northern Dancer, the stallion would die "in the act at the end of the season, having just bred 40 mares. That's the way he would probably want to go."

To which Taylor added the following year: "I didn't say which season, though. Every year a horse at that age has to be on borrowed time. But he's showing no diminution of vigor or desire to breed or whatever. The great thing is some stallions seem to tail off as they get older in terms of their progeny, which may be because they get lesser mares than they got at their prime, but he's doing anything but tailing off."

Northern Dancer was retired from breeding on April 15, 1987. "For about a month prior to that, we began to be concerned about him because we started seeing some of his early mares coming back," Hickey said. "He was always a very 'sure' horse. It just looked like with age he was losing the ability to get the mares in foal. And then right at the end he also lost the desire. He was taxing himself because he was not impregnating the mares, and his mares were coming back, and his workload was increasing, and he wasn't really up to it. So we retired him."

Windfields closed its Maryland breeding operation in 1988, but Northern Dancer, at the age of twenty-seven, was considered too old to move to a new home and, according to Hickey, "will live here with round-the-clock care until he dies."

There may never be another stallion to leave his stamp on the worldwide breeding industry as Northern Dancer did. "He's really left his mark on the breed for all the time to come, I would think," Hickey said in 1988. "I would certainly think that he's the most successful commercial stallion in the history of the breed. He happened to be at the height of his powers at the time the market got so giddy, and he was in a position to capitalize on the rapid escalation of yearling prices. That, coupled with the fact that he was a very closely managed stallion from the very beginning. When he was syndicated in 1970, for instance, there were only 32 shares. Today, the common practice is 40 shares. It's not uncommon for a stallion to be bred to 70 mares, or even more, today, whereas in *no year* of his career did he ever have more than 46 mares. So it not only contributed, we hope, to his longevity, but it also created a special premium on his yearling sales. There weren't ever that many—they were never flooding the market with

Northern Dancer yearlings, so it really put a premium on their value."

On July 18, 1989, when two yearling sons of Northern Dancer entered the ring at the Keeneland July Selected Yearling Sale, it marked the end of an era. These were the last two foals of Northern Dancer, whose breeding season in 1987 was an abbreviated one.

The last two yearlings sold for first $700,000 and later a sales-topping $2.8 million. In concluding his remarks on the latter yearling, the sales announcer said: "The colt is by the legend. He's by Northern Dancer. The end of a legend. He's by Northern Dancer."

The bidding started at $500,000, and when it reached $2.8 million, auctioneer Tom Caldwell said: "Not much we can say that you haven't already thought. He's the last one of The Great." Soon after, the colt reared in the ring, prompting Caldwell to tell the amused crowd: "Look at that, he's performing for you all. Isn't that worth another $50,000?" The crowd applauded.

As soon as Caldwell hammered down his gavel, ending the sale at the $2.8-million mark, applause again rang out in the pavilion.

"Ladies and gentlemen," Caldwell said, "I think we would be remiss if we didn't, in behalf of the great memories that that horse's sire has given us, give a round of applause" to Mr. and Mrs. Charles Taylor. At Caldwell's request, the Taylors stood—and the crowd applauded again. And then the buyer of the yearling, Japanese horseman Zenya Yoshida, also at Caldwell's request, stood to a round of applause.

Gone are the Northern Dancer yearlings, but not the Northern Dancer blood. His sons have proved to be highly successful sires themselves.

"He's a great sire of sires," Hickey said. "And the Northern Dancers didn't have to be particularly brilliant racehorses to be very good sires. His prepotency is the key to the whole thing."

That Northern Dancer sire line is a strong one, an influential one, a lasting one. It stretches to all parts of the globe. To England and Ireland. To France and the Far East. And to New Zealand and Australia. His sons are carrying on at stud in the proud tradition of their father.

As for Northern Dancer, after Windfields vacated the farm in the fall of 1988, it spent more than $80,000 a year to maintain the old horse, seeing to it that he was taken care of properly with round-the-clock attention, until its stallion division in Maryland was purchased in 1990 by the Northview Stallion Station. Northern Dancer remained in his same stall and same paddock at his Maryland residence until his death on November 16, 1990. The twenty-nine-year-old pensioner was put down following a severe attack of colic.

Northern Dancer's remains were taken to Canada, and his body was buried in its entirety in a Windfields Farm cemetery between the barn where he was foaled and the barn where he first stood at stud. It seems only fitting that he would wind up in Canada. Charles Taylor once recalled that winning the Derby was "a national event" in Canada.

"So I think most Canadians would think of Northern Dancer as the first Canadian-bred to win the Kentucky Derby," Taylor said. "Whereas most Europeans would think of him as a great sire."

14

Joe Hirsch:
Gentleman of the Turf

IF YOU WANT TO KEEP UP with Joe Hirsch in the days and weeks leading up to the Kentucky Derby, you better have plenty of early speed, handle any kind of going, and come on strong at the end. In other words, you need to have your running shoes on, stay on top of things at all times, and have endurance to the end.

For years, the prolific executive columnist for *Daily Racing Form* has worked indefatigably for hours on end in providing his readers around the country with the latest developments in his "Derby Doings" dispatches.

His columns are read not only by racing fans but a good many writers as well. Many of his peers pore over his stories carefully for information. Rare is the racing writer who has ever scooped Joe Hirsch on a major story.

It's no exaggeration to say that Hirsch is not only the most famous turf writer in the world but also one of the most well known racing personalities throughout the globe. He not only is reporting on racing, he is very much a part of the sport. He is a celebrity in his own right—and one who hasn't let it go to his head. As established as he is, he's not one to rest on his laurels. Conscientiousness and accuracy are his bywords.

Journalism teachers would be well advised to instruct their students to study Hirsch's methods. He does his job the old-fashioned way—with hard work. On Derby Day, for example, while many other journalists are spending

Joe Hirsch (left) and Jim Bolus, author of Remembering the Derby, *in the Churchill Downs stable area.* (Photo by Dick Martin, Louisville, Kentucky)

the afternoon betting and enjoying themselves in the press box, this dean of American turf writers can be found walking through the box areas, chatting with people, taking notes, soaking up the atmosphere. He then returns to the press box and files a story on the dignitaries on hand on this first Saturday in May at Churchill Downs.

Racing can be an intimidating sport to many writers, and Hirsch is the first one to assist neophyte journalists, introducing them to horsemen and helping them to feel comfortable in the racetrack environment.

Once headlined as the "Gentleman of the Turf," Hirsch is respected and liked at the same time, a rare combination indeed.

What makes Joe Hirsch tick? Why is he considered the world's foremost racing writer? Why is he known as Mr. Derby?

Jack Price, the man who bred and trained 1961 Kentucky Derby winner Carry Back, perhaps summed it up best when he said: "He just loves what he's doing, and I think that's the answer—he loves what he's doing."

Because of his reputation and influence, Hirsch is able to get in touch with inaccessible people who otherwise wouldn't come to the phone for many writers. "Even people like George Widener, he wouldn't talk to *any* newspaperman," Price said. "Bert Mulholland, his trainer, told me he thought it was bad luck. But he'd talk with Joe Hirsch. But the rest of them, he would walk right by them."

Owners, trainers, jockeys, and breeders know that Hirsch won't take advantage of something said in confidence, that he will treat a story fairly, that he will look for the positive side of a situation rather than the negative.

As Price put it, "He editorializes very, very rarely, but when he does, it's with good reason. There isn't anyone who can say anything bad about Joe Hirsch. I don't believe he's got an enemy. He's got that reputation of not hurting anybody. No one that I know of has ever said—in my presence—anything against Joe Hirsch. There'll never be another one like him."

Indeed, Joe Hirsch is one of a kind. A holdover from an earlier time when manners and courtesy meant more than they do now, especially in horse racing (The Sport of Kings), Hirsch has achieved his lofty position by combining hard work with grace. Other writers might work hard, but few, if any, have ever been able to put together such a perfect blend of talent and charm. It's called style, and that's what Joe Hirsch has.

A courtly, refined individual, the tall, dark-haired Hirsch is known to bow slightly from the waist when meeting a lady. Many people perceive sportswriters in "The Odd Couple" mode, boisterous, beer-drinking, and sloppy in appearance, but Hirsch doesn't fill that bill. Even on mornings when the rain is slanting down from the sky and the stable area is muddy from one end to the other, one sure bet is that Joe Hirsch will appear in coat and tie. To be sure, many people have never seen him in anything but such attire.

In this day and age when people call you only when they want something, it's not unheard of to pick up the telephone and hear Hirsch's deep, deliberate voice on the other end in a long-distance call from New York or Florida. Hirsch has to be the busiest person in any press box in America, but he might be calling you just to chat for ten minutes or so, just to say hello, just to see how you're doing. He finds the time to do the little things, and the little things add up to make him the success that he is.

Jack Mann, a veteran racing writer, likes to tell this story about Hirsch: "I always called Joe 'the Grover Whalen of racing.' Grover Whalen was the official greeter of the city of New York. When anybody would come in on a boat, he would greet them. Joe always kinda assumed the role of the official greeter. He was being kind, showing new guys around. He'd find a new guy and say, 'Can I *do* anything for you?' But even if you'd *been* around, as I had for a few years, every once in a while, he'd come around and say, 'Hello, how are you feeling?' And he'd always say, 'Is there anything I can *do* for you?'

"Well, this one day at Aqueduct in 1963, it's one of those $25,000 Wednesday stakes. I was working for the *Herald Tribune*, and we're standing in the winner's circle in the rain waiting to talk to the owner and trainer. Just out of being bored or something, I said just for the hell of it, 'Joe, can I do anything for *you*?' And he leaned over very confidentially—he's that much taller than I am—and he said, 'Yeah, wear a tie in the winner's circle, for Christ sake.'"

Cliff Guilliams, the *Daily Racing Form* chart caller in Kentucky, recalls another Hirsch story. Before the 1990 Derby Trial, Guilliams was standing next to Hirsch on the press box porch at Churchill Downs. The speedy Housebuster was an overwhelming 1–5 favorite in the race.

"Joe," Guilliams said, "you know this horse could probably be on the lead in the Derby and have things his own way."

"Oh, well, don't worry about it," Hirsch said. "Jimmy [Jimmy Croll, the trainer of Housebuster] has already told me he's not going to run him in the Derby no matter what happens."

"Well, let me ask you this," Guilliams said. "What happens if he gets beat today?"

Hirsch looked at Guilliams with a sly grin and replied: "Well, if he gets beat, make sure you hurry back off this porch, because there'll be bodies falling off the top of this grandstand—and you may get hit."

As it turned out, nobody was jumping off the roof following the '90 Trial. Housebuster won by 5¼ lengths.

For years, Hirsch has been the Blue Grass Press Dinner's master of ceremonies at Keeneland. In 1993, he introduced the connections for Wallenda, who was named after famous high-wire walker Karl Wallenda. "This horse was named for a man who made only one mistake in his life."

Pausing, Hirsch added: "Unfortunately, this man was in a profession which didn't allow for *any* mistakes."

The dinner gathering broke up in laughter.

Hirsch, who has covered races throughout America, spends much of the summer and fall in New York, where he has an apartment on the East Side. During the winter, he is headquartered in Miami Springs, Florida. Wherever he's based, he does a good bit of traveling, including two or three trips a year to California.

Hirsch arrives in Kentucky for the Keeneland spring meeting and brings with him many of his personal possessions—clothing, books, and papers. He thrives on covering the Derby, never tiring of the demanding schedule.

"I try to get to the track at 6 and work until 9, 9:30 and then sit down and write," he said. "I write usually from 9 to 3 steadily, because 3 o'clock in the East is 12 o'clock in the West, and that's more or less the deadline for our Western edition. Of course, it's not all writing for six hours. A lot of it is telephoning. And it's kind of a difficult thing to get back on your train of thought after having been interrupted for a phone call. I always have two phones—one incoming and one outgoing—and I try to keep them both busy."

Hirsch has said that there have been years when he would write as many as 8,000 words daily as Derby Day drew near.

In a cover story for *Thoroughbred Racing Action*, Hirsch was asked by writer William Leggett how much he runs up in phone bills during the course of a year. "I wouldn't know," he said. "I've never wanted to know. I have told the office never to tell me."

Hirsch attends the various parties during Derby Week, but he is still up bright and early in the morning. And when the trim, dark-haired Hirsch arrives at the track, it's in coat and tie—and his trademark sunglasses. "Since he is quite tall and carries himself erectly, in the manner of a man who understands the meaning of dignity, Joe is easily distinguishable when he arrives in a stable area," Timothy T. Capps once wrote in *The Thoroughbred Record*. "Trainers and officials greet him warmly, for almost all of them know him, and those who do not at least know who he is. More than 35 years on the racing trail have given Joe the status, if not the age, of an elder statesman of the Turf, particularly about important matters such as the Triple Crown races."

Through the years, Hirsch has covered many a mile in the Churchill Downs stable area. Writing in a small notebook, he touches base with the connections of all the Derby horses. He stops off at this barn to check with D. Wayne Lukas on his Derby hopeful, goes over to that barn to interview Woody Stephens about his colt, and moves on at a brisk gait to talk with Charlie Whittingham. He simply doesn't miss a thing in his morning rounds.

When computers were introduced to journalism, Hirsch chose instead to use a typewriter, but eventually he gave in to the age of automation. Even so, he still is known to rely on a manual typewriter for free-lance stories.

A native of New York, Hirsch first attended the University of New Hampshire and later graduated from New York University's journalism school. He was a stringer for a brief time for *The New York Times*. "That was in '48," he said. "Or nineteen and forty-eight. Some people think I have been around since 1848." He was hired by *The Morning Telegraph* (a now-defunct sister publication to the *Daily Racing Form*) in 1948, working as a deskman and also writing stories about sports other than racing. He then entered the Army in 1950 for a four-year stint, serving as a medical officer in Europe and later going to Washington, where he wrote speeches for generals. After his discharge, he stayed in the reserves for another ten years.

In 1954, following his four years of active duty, he returned to *The Morning Telegraph*. In the spring of that year, he wrote his first racing story, an interview with Tommy Root, Sr., the trainer of sprint champion White Skies. His editors liked the story. "Tommy was a good fellow to interview," Hirsch recalled. "He was very articulate and so forth."

It so happened that at about that time a writer for *The Morning Telegraph* became ill on assignment at Suffolk Downs, a track in Boston, Massachusetts, and "the paper asked me to go up and fill in for a week. It sounded like fun, so I went up. And, of course, I never came back."

Hirsch, who didn't have a racing background as a youth, is quick to credit New England turf writers Gerry Sullivan, Dave Wilson, and John Aborn for the assistance that they gave him when he first went to work at Suffolk Downs. "I didn't really know too much about racing," Hirsch recalled, "and those fellows helped me a great deal. They were a lovely bunch of fellows."

Two years later, Hirsch was sent to Louisville to cover his first Derby, and in time he developed a reputation as the best in the business. Named executive columnist for *Daily Racing Form* in 1974, he has become so widely read that a former racing magazine editor once said of him: "Joe doesn't have to look for things to write about. Everybody in the business is lining up hoping that Joe will write about their horses."

Wrote Jim O'Donnell in the *Daily Herald* (Arlington Heights, Illinois): "His bearing is regal, his knowledge of Thoroughbred racing encyclopedic and when Joe Hirsch talks, all of turfdom listens."

His responsibilities have changed over the years. "In the old days," he said, "it was just writing a column. In recent years, there have been some other things that have taken up a great deal of time, both for the paper and for other things such as the Hall of Fame and what have you."

Unlike most turf writers, Hirsch rarely wagers. And when he does, it's usually just two dollars. A big tipper, Hirsch appreciates fine restaurants and is instantly recognized by maître d's. In Kentucky, his favorite restaurants are Hasenour's in Louisville and The Coach House in Lexington.

Hirsch, a keen sports fan, once roomed with Joe Namath of the New York Jets. "When Joe played, I used to drive him to the game every Sunday and drive him back to the apartment that we shared," Hirsch said. "We lived together for five years when he first came up with the Jets. We were introduced by Sonny Werblin, who at that time was the president of the Jets and also active in the Monmouth Park racetrack."

Hirsch's reputation extends to all parts of the globe. He has covered racing on four continents, including visits to England, Ireland, France, Japan, and South Africa. He wrote a weekly column for *The Sporting Life* (a daily racing publication) in London for thirty-five years but was obliged to give up that assignment because of the differences between publishers Robert Maxwell, who owned *The Sporting Life*, and Rupert Murdoch, who at that time owned *Daily Racing Form*.

Hirsch once headed the American selection committee for the Washington, D.C., International at Laurel Race Course and had a hand in the development of the Arlington Million, an international race inaugurated in 1981.

"He stands heads and shoulders above pressmen on both sides of the Atlantic," said Nick Clarke, managing director of the International Racing Bureau, which has its head office in England. "He's very, very well respected and enormously liked. There's no kinder person than Joe Hirsch. If somebody's stuck for information on what's happening in the States, he's always the first to volunteer information and to help.

"He's always totally aware of what's happening in Europe,

Joe Hirsch (right) with French trainer François Boutin at the 1988 Breeders' Cup, which was run at Churchill Downs. (Photo by Jim Bolus)

Joe Hirsch received the 1992 Eclipse Award of Merit from trainer Charlie Whittingham. (Courtesy Stidham & Associates)

whether it's from a racing point of view, from a breeding point of view, from a gossip point of view," Clarke added. "Joe's very much the racing-writer-man-of-the-world. He does know what's happening. He's very international in his outlook."

Hirsch is on a first-name basis with many European racing people. "Everybody in Europe knows him very well," English jockey Pat Eddery said at the 1989 Breeders' Cup in Florida. "I've known Joe now for a long time. I first met him when I came to New York about 12 years ago, and he's a wonderful guy. I came over for a vacation to Los Angeles about five years ago, and he took me everywhere— all around the place. He took me to Santa Anita, gave me a nice lunch, and he looked after me very well. Very nice man."

Hirsch has been honored many times, including receiving the sport's most prestigious award—the 1992 Eclipse Award of Merit.

He also received a 1981 award in England for services to international racing. He was the first American to receive this award, presented annually by the International Racing Bureau. In addition, he won the coveted Eclipse Award for outstanding newspaper writing in 1978 and in 1989 was the recipient of The Jockey Club Medal, which is presented each year to an individual for outstanding contributions to Thoroughbred racing and breeding. "Joe Hirsch is probably as widely known in racing as any owner or breeder," said Ogden Mills Phipps, chairman of The Jockey Club.

Hirsch also received the 1974 Engelhard Award from the Thoroughbred Breeders of Kentucky, the 1980 Dean Eagle Memorial Award from the Knights of Columbus in Louisville, the 1983 Big Sport of Turfdom Award from the Turf Publicists of America, and the 1984 Walter Haight Award from the National Turf Writers Association. Moreover, he has been honored by the Baltimore Lodge of the

Sons of Italy, which bears his name on a Federico Tesio prize called the Joe Hirsch Pursuit of Excellence Award.

One of the founders of the National Turf Writers Association, Hirsch was the organization's first president (1959–60). Despite his busy daily schedule with *Daily Racing Form*, Hirsch has found time to turn out four books, two that he wrote himself (*The Grand Senor: The Fabulous Career Of Horatio Luro* and *A Treasury of Questions and Answers from* The Morning Telegraph *and* Daily Racing Form) and two that he coauthored (*Kentucky Derby: The Chance of a Lifetime* and *In the Winner's Circle: The Jones Boys of Calumet Farm*).

Hirsch also is a trustee of the National Museum of Racing and chairman of racing's Hall of Fame committee.

He has been around a long time, and his age has been a matter of conjecture in racing circles. He appeared at a Bill Shoemaker Charity Celebrity Roast in Oklahoma in December 1989, and the veteran jockey said of Hirsch: "No one knows for sure how old Joe is, but the first race story he wrote was on Ben-Hur."

Reminded of Shoemaker's Ben-Hur comment, Hirsch replied in an interview later that month, "You might say that I don't remember that race very well. Besides, it's chariot racing. He must have made a mistake. I never covered chariot racing in my life."

Hirsch, who turned sixty-five in 1993, was asked in 1990 about retirement. "I haven't really had much time to think about that," he said. "I guess in 20 or 30 years I'll have to give it serious thought."

Hirsch has covered every Derby since 1956. He shared a room that year in the Brown Hotel with jockey Bill Hartack, who won the '56 Kentucky Oaks on Princess Turia and then finished second in the Derby on Fabius. "He went over to the turf writers' dinner with me and cleaned out most of the guys in a crap game or a poker game afterward," Hirsch recalled.

No writer can comment better on the magic of the Derby than Hirsch. "The fascinating part of it for me is to see the development of the three-year-olds and watch the best riders and trainers," he said. "The mystique of the Derby is that it brings horses from all over together for the first time."

"The name of the game is unpredictability. That's much of the fascination of the Derby. There's always a fresh pack of players. All the horses are different each year, and many of the trainers and jockeys are, too.

"It's like the first marriage; it's the one everybody remembers. When you finish with the Derby and go on to the other Triple Crown events, it's like the honeymoon is over. You get back home, and it's all old hat."

The 1964 Derby was special to Hirsch. That race brought together a memorable matchup—Northern Dancer against Hill Rise. Northern Dancer, the second choice owned by E. P. Taylor and trained by Horatio Luro, edged the favored Hill Rise by a neck in a thrilling battle, and in 1989 Hirsch reflected on the race. "It was a classic confrontation in every respect: The Good Big Horse against the Good Little Horse in the 90th Kentucky Derby, 25 years ago," he wrote. "When it was over, with a dramatic climax that whipped the large crowd to a frenzy, the Good Little Horse, Northern Dancer, emerged with all the spoils. He set a track record of 2:00 for the mile and a quarter, became the first Canadian-bred to win the Run for the Roses and laid the foundation for a sire line that is today the most successful in the world."

Of Northern Dancer, Hirsch once said: "He had a tremendous personality, and just being around him and his connections was a great pleasure. Horatio Luro, of course, was one of the greatest of trainers, and Mr. Taylor was one of racing's truest sportsmen."

Other horses stand out in Hirsch's memory, including Arts and Letters and Tim Tam.

Hirsch said Arts and Letters "was a very good racehorse and could have won the Triple Crown in 1969. He lost the Kentucky Derby by a neck and the Preakness by a head to Majestic Prince. The two rides that Bill Hartack put up on Majestic Prince were two of his greatest. Arts and Letters won the Metropolitan and the Belmont, and after that he took the Jim Dandy, Travers, Woodward, and Jockey Club Gold Cup in order."

Hirsch said Tim Tam "had great tenacity and always seemed to get up and win. He had won 10 races in 1958 before he broke down in the Belmont after winning the first two legs of the Triple Crown. He finished second in the Belmont on a broken leg."

The Derby evokes many pleasant memories for Hirsch, truly a man who has found happiness in his occupation. "I consider myself a very lucky fellow to enjoy doing something as much as I enjoy covering racing," he said. "I just have enjoyed not only racing but the Derby particularly. It's something special. There's a great story every year. It's like a spring festival. It's an enjoyable time every year. It's a great joy to cover, a great feeling of exultation."

Spoken like a man who wouldn't trade places with anybody in the racing world . . . this Gentleman of the Turf.

15

The Stormy Career
of Ed Corrigan

ED CORRIGAN, THE OWNER OF 1890 Kentucky Derby winner Riley, was a troublemaker and a bully. That's when he was in a good mood.

When he was in a bad mood, he was a holy terror, a vicious-tempered man capable of anything short of homicide.

Known as the "stormy petrel" of the American turf, he was a fierce competitor who didn't mind speaking his mind or putting up his fists. He certainly would never have won a personality contest. One person perhaps summarized Corrigan's temperament best by saying: "Ed has an even disposition. He's always mad."

Longtime Churchill Downs boss Col. Matt Winn, in his book *Down the Stretch*, described Corrigan as "a fiery, dynamic Chicago Irishman" and added: "If Ed liked you, he would knock down twenty men to please you; if he didn't, he would knock you down twenty times, just to keep in practice."

Everybody has good points and bad points, and there was a positive side to Corrigan. Winn praised this turfman as a person who wasn't afraid to spend money and who helped people down on their luck. Moreover, Corrigan was a loyal friend, in Winn's words.

The Spirit of the Times said of Corrigan in 1900: "But while aggressive to his foes and absolutely unknown to fear, he is thoroughly loyal to his friends, is true as steel,

Ed Corrigan (right), shown in 1905, started five horses in the Ken-tucky Derby. His Riley triumphed in 1890; Huron and Corsini ran second in 1892 and 1899, respectively; Phil Dwyer was third in 1892; and Irish Pat was an also-ran in 1885. (Courtesy Keeneland-Cook)

and has that golden quality of the true sportsman, the ability to meet the frowns of fortune without a murmur. His worst enemy has never questioned his honesty or integrity."

Corrigan had his share of enemies, to be sure. A brawler, he was always fighting with somebody—a racetrack operator, a starter, a trainer, an owner, a jockey, a groom, a journalist. Col. Phil T. Chinn, a famous old-time turfman, said that Corrigan "enjoyed a fight more than winning a big race or a huge bet."

The notorious Corrigan's fights were well documented through the years.

At the Louisville Jockey Club's 1887 spring meeting, *The Louisville Times* reported that "Corrigan had a difficulty with a boy named George Fish at the track, and the turfman slapped the rider in the face. Fish left swearing vengeance, and some hours afterward Corrigan caught a boy named Adams, who was following him, thinking he was Fish, and choked him. Officer Ferguson interfered and further trouble was prevented."

The Louisville Commercial reported the incident a bit differently, saying that Corrigan "slapped Jockey Adams and Adams went off and got a gun, went back, and asked Corrigan to slap him again, using rather vigorous language in making his request. Corrigan silently declined, and afterwards was under the stand in the barroom when he got into a quarrel with one of the owners of the great Egmont, whom he knocked down and accused of having a pistol. Wash Ferguson, the private policeman, was on hand, and was asked by Corrigan to search the man. He did not do so to the satisfaction of Corrigan, who told him he had not done his duty."

Nowadays, somebody might call a newspaper's ombudsman to complain about a story, but Corrigan had his own way of handling such matters. In 1887, he brutally attacked Thomas A. Mosier, a sportswriter for the *Kansas*

City Times over an article that displeased him. According to one account, the tall, heavy Corrigan struck Mosier, a man of slight build, "a fearful blow in the face, felling him to the ground. He then kicked him several times. Mosier was rendered unconscious, and Corrigan thought he had killed him. He hurriedly dashed a bucket of water upon Mosier, who revived and rose up. Corrigan's anger then returned, and he again assaulted Mosier, kicking him about the body. The witnesses of the assault then interfered. Mosier's right jaw was broken, his head badly cut and bruised, and there was evidence of internal injuries."

The newspaper published an editorial about the assault, unmercifully denouncing Corrigan. The following month in Kansas City, the horseman met up with editor Dr. Morrison Munford of the *Kansas City Times*. Corrigan wasn't interested in debating the issue with Munford. Instead, he attacked the editor. Munford suffered a bruised and blackened right eye. In addition, his head was cut in two places, and the side of his face was hurt. "The papers have all been giving me hell," Corrigan told a reporter for the *Kansas City Star*. "The papers have all treated me dirty."

In 1888 at Chicago's West Side Park, a track in which he had become a managing partner, Corrigan attacked an owner named Samuel Lavis, who had the audacity to complain about the starter. Swinging his cane with full force, Corrigan hit Lavis on the head. Lavis fell, "the blood streaming over his face and clothes," reported *The Courier-Journal*. "Since the races have been opened Corrigan has been the fear of all who have been brought in contact with him. A few days ago he struck a track employee, fracturing his jaw; he has had innumerable encounters with newspaper reporters with whose accounts of the races he had become displeased, and only yesterday threatened to break the head of one of them."

In 1896, Corrigan was stabbed at Latonia by John Phillips, a groom he had ordered fired. Phillips was reputed to be a killer, allegedly having murdered two men in Tennessee, and by all accounts Corrigan was lucky to survive this incident. Phillips was said to be using "an ugly looking knife." Corrigan, who reportedly "was armed only with an umbrella and protected himself as best he could," came away with a severe cut four inches long on his left arm. As for Phillips, *The Louisville Commercial* reported after the incident that the groom escaped and was in hiding in the bushes.

In 1896, after his favored Moylan had lost a race in St. Louis, Corrigan accused the starter, Kit Chinn, of "having thrown the race to Damocles [the winner]," according to *The Thoroughbred Record* magazine. "Corrigan is absolutely without fear, and the Chinns have a record as fighters. Serious trouble was looked for, but the men finally separated without getting together in earnest."

The magazine couldn't help but add this barb: "The Master of Hawthorne will do well to leave young Chinn alone, for when he tackles the Bluegrass boy he will find out that he is not cuffing any of the weak, half-starved stable boys whom he has been in the habit of kicking about whenever his fancy dictated."

By 1905, Corrigan had reached the status of a senior citizen. But had he mellowed? It's doubtful that apprentice jockey Hardwick thought so. The 63-year-old Corrigan was arrested after assaulting Hardwick in the Latonia paddock. Corrigan reportedly "seized the boy by the ears, pulling and twisting them, and reprimanded him" for galloping the mare Alma Dufour too fast in her warm-up for a race.

When it came to keeping trainers, Corrigan was the Elizabeth Arden Graham of his era. Mrs. Graham, owner of 1947 Derby winner Jet Pilot, was famous for hiring and firing trainers, and Corrigan similarly made job security with him akin to walking through a revolving door—here today, gone tomorrow. An 1895 dispatch noted that

Corrigan had "doubtless employed more jockeys and trainers than any other man on the American turf. As a rule, a trainer does not suit him well enough to remain a year. . . ."

Corrigan, primarily an owner who did some training on the side, also campaigned the great filly Modesty, winner of the Kentucky Oaks in 1884 and the inaugural American Derby later that season; Freeland, a gallant gelding; Ban Fox; Irish Pat; Strathmeath; Free Knight; Huron; Phil Dwyer; and Isaac Murphy.

Besides racing horses, Corrigan built Hawthorne Park in Chicago and was involved in the ownership of other tracks as well. While at Hawthorne, Corrigan precipitated a bitter—and bloody—turf war with rival track Garfield Park that resulted in several killings, including the deaths of two policemen.

Corrigan, who amassed and lost several fortunes during his life, sold his horses in 1908 at Lexington, Kentucky, receiving just $22,995 for ninety-two head. Among the horses he sold was McGee ($1,300), whom he had brought over from England. McGee later would sire Kentucky Derby winners Donerail (1913) and Exterminator (1918).

In 1909, Corrigan filed a bankruptcy petition. Gone was the fortune of a man who had once owned (or leased) more than 100 Thoroughbreds in training, who had owned a 503-acre breeding farm in Kentucky, and who had interests in a number of racetracks in America.

In 1914, Corrigan showed up at the Empire track, the first time he had attended the races in more than three years. He was then in the contracting business in Kansas City, Missouri, where his family had moved in 1860. He and his brothers made money (and plenty of it) as pioneers in building the Kansas City Street Railway system. Corrigan later went into the Thoroughbred business, enjoying success through the years as an owner and breeder but losing money as a racetrack proprietor.

In 1915, he made a comeback in the Thoroughbred breeding business. But things didn't get much, if any, better for Corrigan in subsequent years, and he died penniless on July 4, 1924, in Kansas City. He was eighty-two.

A *Turf and Sport Digest* story, written by Horace Wade, summarized Corrigan's final years in this fashion: "His last days were peculiarly pathetic. When he was past seventy he married a young girl of seventeen, the daughter of a carpenter who had once worked at Hawthorne. She soon tired of his overbearing manner and one day eloped with the milkman. . . .

"After this domestic tragedy Corrigan made a feeble effort to stage a comeback. Finally, broken in health and pocket, the former mighty magnate of the turf drifted to a despairing end. The last time the turf saw him he was perched on a feed box during the fall meeting at Beulah Park at Columbus, Ohio, watching the races. From Columbus he drifted to Akron where he was taken sick. Relatives came to his rescue, paying his passage to Kansas City, at which point he died."